THE GOOD NEWS

Norval F. Pease

THE GOOD NEWS

Thirteen Vital Points of Faith

Review and Herald Publishing Association
Washington, D.C. 20012

Copyright © 1982
by the Review and Herald Publishing Association

Editor: Thomas A. Davis
Design: Alan Forquer
Cover Design: Robert Wright

Bible texts credited to T.E.V. are from the *Good News Bible*—Old Testament: Copyright © American Bible Society 1976; New Testament: Copyright © American Bible Society 1966, 1971, 1976.
Scripture quotations marked R.S.V. are from the *Revised Standard Version of the Bible,* copyrighted 1946, 1952 © 1971, 1973.
Texts credited to N.I.V. are from *The Holy Bible: New International Version.* Copyright © 1978 by the New York International Bible Society. Used by permission of Zondervan Bible Publishers.
Texts credited to N.E.B. are from *The New English Bible.* © The Delegates of the Oxford University Press and the Syndics of the Cambridge University Press 1961, 1970. Reprinted by permission.
Bible texts credited to Phillips are from J. B. Phillips: *The New Testament in Modern English,* Revised Edition. © J. B. Phillips 1958, 1960, 1972. Used by permission of Macmillan Publishing Co., Inc.
Verses marked T.L.B. are taken from *The Living Bible,* copyright 1971 by Tyndale House Publishers, Wheaton, Ill. Used by permission.

Library of Congress Cataloging in Publication Data

Pease, Norval F.
 The good news.

 1. Seventh-Day Adventists—Catechisms and creeds—English. 2. Seventh-Day Adventists—Doctrinal and controversial works. I. Title.
BX6154.P38   1982   238'.673   82-15155
ISBN 0-8280-0157-X

Printed in U.S.A.

Contents

I   GOOD NEWS ABOUT GOD   9
"Do you believe in God the Father, in His Son Jesus Christ, and in the Holy Spirit?"

II   GOOD NEWS FROM CALVARY   20
"Do you accept the death of Jesus Christ on Calvary as the atoning sacrifice for the sins of men, and believe that through faith in His shed blood men are saved from sin and its penalty?"

III   GOOD NEWS ABOUT SALVATION   28
"Renouncing the world and its sinful ways, have you accepted Jesus as your personal Saviour, and do you believe that God, for Christ's sake, has forgiven your sins and given you a new heart?"

IV   GOOD NEWS ABOUT OUR FRIEND IN HEAVEN   37
"Do you accept by faith the righteousness of Christ, recognizing Him as your Intercessor in the heavenly sanctuary, and do you claim His promise to strengthen you by His indwelling Spirit, so that you may receive power to do His will?"

V   GOOD NEWS ABOUT THE BIBLE   45
"Do you believe that the Bible is God's inspired word, and that it constitutes the only rule of faith and practice for the Christian?"

VI   GOOD NEWS FROM SINAI   54
"Do you accept the Ten Commandments as still binding upon Christians; and is it your purpose, by the power of the indwelling Christ, to keep this law, including the fourth commandment, which requires the observance of the seventh day of the week as the Sabbath of the Lord?"

VII   GOOD NEWS ABOUT THE RETURN OF JESUS   65
"Is the soon coming of Jesus the blessed hope in your heart, and are you determined to be personally ready to meet the Lord, and to do all in your power to witness to His loving salvation, and by life and word to help others to be ready for His glorious appearing?"

VIII   GOOD NEWS ABOUT GOD'S GIFTS   78
"Do you accept the Biblical teaching of spiritual gifts, and do you believe the gift of prophecy in the remnant church is one of the identifying marks of that church?"

IX   GOOD NEWS ABOUT THE CHURCH   86
                     AND ITS MISSION

"Do you believe in church organization, and is it your purpose to support the church by your tithes and offerings, your personal effort, and influence?"

X   GOOD NEWS ABOUT THE BODY   94
                        GOD GAVE YOU

"Do you believe that your body is the temple of the Holy Spirit and that you are to honor God by caring for your body, avoiding the use of that which is harmful, abstaining from all unclean foods, from the use, manufacture, or sale of alcoholic beverages, the use, manufacture, or sale of tobacco in any of its forms for human consumption, and from the misuse of, or trafficking in, narcotics or other drugs?"

XI   GOOD NEWS ABOUT CHRISTIAN LIFE STYLE   102

"Knowing and understanding the fundamental Bible principles, as taught by the Seventh-day Adventist Church, is it your purpose, by the grace of God, to order your life in harmony with these principles?"

XII   GOOD NEWS ABOUT BAPTISM   110

"Do you accept the New Testament teaching of baptism by immersion, and do you desire to be so baptized as a public expression of your faith in Christ and in the forgiveness of your sins?"

XIII   GOOD NEWS ABOUT THE CHURCH AS A PLACE   117
                OF WORSHIP AND FELLOWSHIP

"Do you believe that the Seventh-day Adventist Church is the remnant church of Bible prophecy, and that people of every nation, race, and language are invited and accepted into its fellowship? Do you desire membership in this local congregation of the world church?"

Preface

When a person presents himself for membership in the Seventh-day Adventist Church, he is expected to say Yes to a series of questions known as the baptismal vow. These questions are printed on his baptismal certificate, and are copied from a book called the *Seventh-day Adventist Church Manual.*

The questions differ from a formal creed in that they are not part of a church liturgy. They are not published in a prayer book or memorized by the prospective member or repeated at a church service. Their purpose is to acquaint the new Adventist with the basic beliefs held by his church. This list of beliefs is formulated and approved by the General Conference of the church in regular session. Any revisions must be voted by the same body. This book is based on the 1980 revision.

The thirteen chapters of this book deal with the thirteen statements of doctrine included in the baptismal vow. These chapters are intended not as exhaustive theological treatises, but as practical discussions.

The title of this book is significant. Every doctrine that an Adventist or any other Christian is expected to believe must be a part of the "good news." Ever since Pentecost, Christians have been proclaiming the gospel of a crucified, risen, and returning Saviour. Adventists are endeavoring to announce this age-old good news in a unique setting—the setting of a world that is soon (though we do not know just *how* soon) going to meet its Judge and Saviour.

There are three scriptural passages that Adventists take very seriously:

"And this Good News about the Kingdom will be preached through all the world for a witness to all mankind; and then the end will come" (Matt. 24:14, T.E.V.).

"Go, then, to all peoples everywhere and make them my disciples: baptize them in the name of the Father, the Son, and the Holy Spirit, and teach them to obey everything I have commanded you. And I will be with you always, to the end of the age" (chap. 28:19, 20, T.E.V.).

"Then I saw another angel [messenger] flying high in the air, with an eternal message of Good News to announce to the peoples of the earth, to every race, tribe, language, and nation" (Rev. 14:6, T.E.V.).

The good news preached at Pentecost has never lost its relevance. It was intended for *all* mankind, and it was to be proclaimed until the divine Author of the good news should return.

Some readers may ask, "What is distinctive about the Seventh-day Adventist understanding of the good news? Is it the Sabbath? Or the Second Coming? Or the nature of man? Or a different life style? Or the gift of prophecy? Or the unique mission of the church?" The distinctiveness of Adventism is found in the unique *blend* of the doctrines described in *all thirteen* of the questions asked of the baptismal candidate. These doctrines are like thirteen links in a chain. The good news is not complete if any one is omitted. All are centered in Christ and all are intended to show how a person can *become* a Christian, how he can *be* a Christian, and how he can finally be among the redeemed in the kingdom of God.

For the author this is more than just another book. It is a confession of faith. And it is his hope that these pages will either persuade or remind *you* that God has good news for *you*.

Norval F. Pease
Grand Terrace, California

CHAPTER I

Good News About God

"Do you believe in God the Father, in His Son Jesus Christ, and in the Holy Spirit?"

THIS IS the first question asked of a candidate for baptism into the Seventh-day Adventist Church. Why should this question precede all others? The answer is suggested in the Great Commission that Jesus gave to His followers:

"'Go therefore and make disciples of all nations, baptizing them *in the name of the Father and of the Son and of the Holy Spirit;* teaching them to observe all that I have commanded you; and lo, I am with you always, to the close of the age'" (Matt. 28:19, 20, R.S.V.).

The expression "in the name of" may mean either "into the family of" or "by the authority of." In either case, the newly baptized person must "believe" for the rite of baptism to have any meaning. This "belief" must include acceptance of God as the heavenly Father, of Jesus Christ as Lord and Saviour, and of the Holy Spirit as Helper and Guide. This expression of faith is basic to being a Seventh-day Adventist Christian. It must precede everything else.

10 / THE GOOD NEWS

The good news about God is, first of all, that His love, His grace, His forgiveness, and His salvation, are available as a free gift for all. But for each to receive the gift, he must believe it is for him, and accept it..

The good news also includes the sacrifice of His Son, and the ministry of the Holy Spirit. The newly baptized believer has experienced a *new birth* and is introduced into a *new life.* This is the thrilling consequence of believing in the Father, the Son, and the Holy Spirit. This is the substance of the Christian's faith.

Let us pause to think about the idea of three "persons" in the heavenly trio. Why should there be a "Father," a "Son," and a "Holy Spirit"? How can we say that we worship one God when we apply the term "God" to three "persons"? This problem has baffled Christians for two thousand years. Someone has said, "He who would try to understand the Trinity fully will lose his mind. But he who would deny the Trinity will lose his soul."—Harold Lindsell and Charles J. Woodbridge, *A Handbook of Christian Truth,* pp. 51, 52.

While none of us can "understand the Trinity fully," we can employ a few analogies that may be helpful. Did you ever know three persons who completely agreed on every point, who understood one another perfectly, who had identically the same objectives and concerns? The best possible marriage never produced this degree of unity. No two friends—let alone three—were ever in such complete agreement. Not even identical twins could fit this pattern. The Father, the Son, and the Holy Spirit are one in purpose, in mind, in character (*The Ministry of Healing,* p. 422) in a manner that no two or more human beings can experience.

It must be remembered that all three persons of the Trinity existed from all eternity, all three possess all the attributes of Deity, and all three are involved in the salvation of mankind. "God" has been defined as the "family name." We are baptized in the "name" (not the "names") of the Father, the Son, and the Holy Spirit; and that name is God. A mystery? Yes. Billy Graham has suggested that the doctrine of the Trinity cannot be described by the equation $1 + 1 + 1 = 1$, but rather by $1 \times 1 \times 1 = 1$. But after all the Christian thought of twenty centuries, the Trinity remains a mystery that must be accepted by faith.

What can we say about God the Father that has not already been said? Probably nothing. But we can remind ourselves of the nature of the God in whom we have believed. I have been helped by a statement in the *Seventh-day Adventist Bible Dictionary:*

"God is portrayed as One who demands much but gives freely. He expects obedience, but pays an infinite price to make obedience possible. He has an immutable law, but He supplies inexhaustible grace. He hates sin with bitter hatred, but loves the sinner with wonderful love. He is the Creator and sustainer of the limitless universe, yet He is the anxious father waiting at the gate for the prodigal's return. He challenges the intellect of the most brilliant men the world has known, yet He accepts the devotion of a little child. Jesus referred to Him as merciful, concerned about human needs, generous, loving, spiritual."—Page 407. Should it be hard to believe in a God like that?

Yet there are many honest, dedicated Christians who have been misled to believe that this loving God maintains a "concentration camp" somewhere in the universe where He imprisons lost souls for eternity. From Greek philosophy, early Christianity borrowed the idea of the natural immortality of the soul. The logical conclusion of this mistaken doctrine was that those who are not saved to enjoy eternal bliss are lost to live in eternal despair.

Some have painted lurid pictures of flames, pitchforks, and demons; others are content to picture being lost as "separation from God." Whatever the temperature of the abode of the damned, Christians who believe in soul immortality agree that their damnation lasts for eternity.

Such teaching is at variance with everything the Bible has to say about God. It is true that God judges, but His judgments are merciful, not cruel. He will eventually destroy sin and sinners. But He will not perpetuate evil in a place of torment worse than any holocaust conceived by mortal maniacs.

What can we say about Jesus, the Son, that has not already been said? Probably nothing. But we can remind ourselves of the kind of Lord we love and serve.

First of all, we think of Him as the God-man. This is a mystery. The Lord Jesus Christ, the divine Son of God, existed from eternity, a distinct person, yet one with the Father. How could such a Being assume the limitations of humanity, yet maintain His identity as the Son of God? The "Incarnation," as it is called, is best described in the magnificent poem of Philippians 2:5-11:
"Your attitude should be the same as that of Christ Jesus:
   Who, being in the very nature God,
      did not consider equality with God
         something to be grasped,
   but made himself nothing,
      taking the very nature of a servant,
      being made in human likeness.
   And being found in appearance as a man,
      he humbled himself
      and became obedient to death—
         even death on a cross!

> Therefore God exalted him to the highest place
>   And gave him the name that is above every name,
>   that at the name of Jesus every knee should bow,
>   in heaven and on earth and under the earth,
>   and every tongue confess that Jesus Christ is Lord,
>   to the glory of God the Father" (N.I.V.).

What kind of a God-man resulted from this act of unfathomable divine love? He is described this way in one book:

"Our Lord fed the five thousand miraculously; yet He knew the pangs of hunger. He dispensed the water of life; yet He thirsted beside a Samaritan well. He stilled the troubled waves of the Sea of Galilee; yet He slept in a little boat. He spoke and Lazarus was loosed from the shackles of death; yet He wept when He heard that His friend had died. An earthquake occurred at His death; yet on the cross He experienced the piercing agony of human pain. Clearly He was both human and divine."—Lindsell and Woodbridge, *op. cit.,* pp. 57, 58.

The following suggestions may help enrich our understanding of Jesus:

1. Let us avoid nit-picking arguments about the divine-human nature of Jesus. We will never—in this life, at least—fully understand how He differed from us and how He was like us. Yet we can *believe* in Him, our divine-human Lord, with all our heart.

2. Let us resist the humanistic trend to consider Jesus merely as an example. True, He is our perfect example, but He is also our Saviour. It would be very discouraging to have an example like Jesus if we did not have a Saviour like Jesus.

3. Let us not overlook the great themes of Jesus' teaching, such as "The Kingdom of God," "The Higher Righteousness," "True Greatness," "Saving the Lost,"

"The Bread of Life," "The Holy Spirit," "The Second Coming," "Proper Law Observance," "Christian Love."

4. Let us remember that Jesus' miracles are our finest lessons on faith. Almost every healing narrative says something about believing: "Believe only, and she [Jairus' daughter] shall be made whole" (Luke 8:50) and "He [a blind man] said, Lord, I believe" (John 9:38).

5. In studying the parables of Jesus, let us try to discover the lesson Jesus meant to convey to those who were listening to Him. Let us not dream up applications that were not intended and might be misleading.

6. Let us listen for the theme of salvation that was emphasized by all of the writers of the Gospels. They were more than biographers—they were preachers of the good news.

7. Let us never overlook the importance of Jesus' death and resurrection. More than one fourth of the Gospels is devoted to this part of the story. The cross and the open tomb were absolutely essential to the fulfillment of His mission. Jesus came to die and to rise again.

What is the central theme of the story of Jesus? It is *love*. Paul said it with thrilling eloquence:

"Who shall separate us from the *love* of Christ? shall tribulation, or distress, or persecution, or famine, or nakedness, or peril, or sword? As it is written, For thy sake we are killed all the day long; we are accounted as sheep for the slaughter. Nay, in all these things we are more than conquerors through him that *loved* us. For I am persuaded, that neither death, nor life, nor angels, nor principalities, nor powers, nor things present, nor things to come, nor height, nor depth, nor any other creature, shall be able to separate us from the *love* of God, which is in Christ Jesus our Lord" (Rom. 8:35-39).

What can we say about the Holy Spirit that has not

GOOD NEWS ABOUT GOD / 15

already been said? Probably nothing. But we can remind ourselves of the relevance of the Christian doctrine that God, in the person of His Spirit, is always at our side.

Jesus' great promise of the Holy Spirit is found in John 14:16: "And I will pray the Father, and he shall give you another Comforter, that he may abide with you for ever."

The meaning of this promise is enriched and clarified by comparing several translations:

Good News Bible: " 'I will ask the Father, and he will give you another *Helper,* who will stay with you forever.' "

Revised Standard Version: " 'And I will pray the Father, and he will give you another *Counselor,* to be with you for ever.' "

The New English Bible: " 'I will ask the Father, and he will give you another to be your *Advocate,* who will be with you for ever—the Spirit of truth.' "

J. B. Phillips: " 'I shall ask the Father to give you *Someone else to stand by you,* to be with you always. I mean the Spirit of truth.' "

"Comforter," "Helper," "Counselor," "Advocate," "Someone else to stand by you"—these are various ways of describing the work of the Holy Spirit. Phillips probably captured the thought of the original text most accurately. Jesus had "stood by" His disciples. Now He was leaving. He was asking His Father to send " 'Someone else to stand by' " them, and that " 'Someone else' " was the Holy Spirit. He was to come to comfort, help, counsel, and defend. And He was to remain " 'forever.' "

In this passage we see the Trinity at work in man's behalf. *Jesus* prays *the Father,* who sends the *Holy Spirit.* The Father, the Son, and the Holy Spirit work together for the salvation of the world. It is equally true to say "Jesus saves," "the Father saves," "the Holy Spirit saves."

When the candidate for baptism affirms that he

believes in the Father, Son, and Holy Spirit, he is doing more than acknowledging that They exist and should be recognized. Belief means acceptance, trust, and commitment.

The psalmist caught this idea when he said, "O God, thou art *my* God" (Ps. 63:1). It is not enough to have an intellectual appreciation of the Father, the Son, and the Holy Spirit. It is not enough to talk about God in an abstract way. My goal must be to reach the place where *I* can say with the psalmist, "Thou art *my* God."

There are numerous Biblical examples of the proper relationship between a person and his God. A few selected incidents may help us to understand.

The apostle Paul had an affliction which he described as "a painful physical ailment" (2 Cor. 12:7, T.E.V.). What did he do about it? There wasn't much medical help available in Paul's day, but there was One to whom he could take his problem. "Three times I prayed to the Lord about this and asked him to take it away" (verse 8, T.E.V.).

What was God's response?

" 'My grace is all you need, for my power is strongest when you are weak' " (verse 9, T.E.V.).

Paul accepted this bad news: "I am most happy, then, to be proud of my weaknesses, in order to feel the protection of Christ's power over me" (verse 9, T.E.V.).

Paul knew how to talk to his Lord, and he knew how to accept the response. Paul could have joined the psalmist in saying, "Thou art *my* God."

This close relationship with God was also revealed in the Old Testament. One of the best examples is found in the experience of Abraham. One day Abraham's God gave him a very disquieting message. God said, " 'Leave your native land, your relatives, and your father's home,

GOOD NEWS ABOUT GOD / 17

and go to a country that I am going to show you' " (Gen. 12:1, T.E.V.).

God softened the blow by giving Abraham a promise: " 'I will give you many descendants, and they will become a great nation. I will bless you and make your name famous, so that you will be a blessing. I will bless those who bless you, but I will curse those who curse you. And through you I will bless all the nations' " (verses 2, 3, T.E.V.).

The Old Testament records several instances when God repeated this promise to Abraham. In each instance, the patriarch needed a lift. For example, God appeared to him when he reached the land to which he had been led. Abraham was homesick and surrounded by enemies. But God said, " 'This is the country that I am going to give to your descendants' " (verse 7, T.E.V.).

The next record we have of God's repetition of the promise was after Abraham's nephew Lot had left him. Abraham had been saddened by the conflict between his men and Lot's men. He was also concerned about Lot's choice of a new location. In this time of stress, God returned with His familiar promise.

Later, Abraham became involved in a military engagement in an effort to rescue Lot from the results of his unwise move. Following his defeat of the enemy, Abraham began to worry that they might plan vengeance. Again he heard the familiar voice, " 'Look at the sky and try to count the stars; you will have as many descendants as that' " (chap. 15:5, T.E.V.).

Abraham was human and became involved in a marital situation that resulted in tension and heartache. No doubt he regretted his mistake keenly, but his Friend didn't forsake him. Again, the familiar voice, " 'I am the Almighty God. Obey me and always do what is right. I will make my covenant with you and give you many descendants'" (chap. 17:1, 2, T.E.V.).

Finally, Abraham proved his absolute commitment to his God, and his divine Friend was there to commend him: "All the nations will ask me to bless them as I have blessed your descendants—all because you obeyed my command" (chap. 22:18, T.E.V.).

The same gracious heavenly Father remembered His Son, Jesus, at the crisis hours of His life. The Gospels record three occasions when Jesus heard the audible voice of His Father. The first was at His baptism, just before He endured the temptations in the desert. The second was at the Transfiguration, just as He was losing popular acclaim in Galilee, and starting His journey that He knew would take Him to the cross. The third was in the Temple court during the last week before Gethsemane and the cross.

Mankind has been described as a kindergarten, trying to spell "God" with the wrong blocks. Some people see God as a life force, a first cause, a universal mind. But this isn't enough. Others see God in nature, in beauty, and in great ideals. This is good, but not good enough. There are others who see God as Creator, lawgiver, ruler, judge, and king. He is all of these, but much more. *Jesus came to teach us that God is our Father, Jesus is our Saviour, and the Holy Spirit is our Helper.*

It isn't enough for the Seventh-day Adventist Christian—or any Christian—to know *about* God. He must know God. And the prerequisite for *knowing* God is *faith*. When the new Christian says "I believe," he is opening the door for a relationship that will transform his life. He is plugging in to a source of power that will bring companionship, security, understanding, victory, and hope.

> "That thou shoulds't think so much of me,
>   And be the God thou art
> Is darkness to my intellect
>   But sunshine to my heart."
>   —Faber

CHAPTER II

Good News From Calvary

"Do you accept the death of Jesus Christ on Calvary as the atoning sacrifice for the sins of men, and believe that through faith in His shed blood men are saved from sin and its penalty?"

WHAT DOES it mean to "accept the death of Jesus Christ on Calvary as the atoning sacrifice"? Christians have been debating this question for two thousand years. Numerous theories have been preached and published in an effort to explain "the atonement."

We will introduce this subject by a quotation from the *Seventh-day Adventist Encyclopedia* in order to summarize what Seventh-day Adventists in general mean when they say "atonement."

"Theologically atonement is the process by which a sinner is reconciled to God or brought into a state of at-one-ment with Him. Christ's vicarious sacrifice upon the cross is the central, decisive, effective act in this process, and without it all else would be insufficient to atone for sin. The atonement there provided was perfect and complete. It was 'once for all' in the sense that it would never have to be repeated. Having made the atonement on the cross, Christ ascended to heaven as our great high priest, there to be our intercessor and to minister on our behalf the benefits of the atonement made available at the cross. . . . Since His ascension, Christ ever lives to make intercession for us, and this intercession is part of the work of reconciliation, or atonement, in its larger sense. . . . Accordingly, He invites us to draw near to the throne of grace with confidence, 'that we may obtain mercy, and find grace to help in time of need' (Heb. 4:16)."—Page 94.

The two quotations that follow suggest the atoning Christ on the cross and risen in glory.

"The atonement of Christ was not made in order to induce God to love those whom He otherwise hated; it was not made to produce a love that was not in existence; but it was made as a manifestation of the love that was already in God's heart."—Ellen G. White, in *Signs of the Times,* May 30, 1895.

"The great Sacrifice had been offered and had been accepted, and the Holy Spirit which descended on the day of Pentecost carried the minds of the disciples from the earthly sanctuary to the heavenly, where Jesus had entered by His own blood, to shed upon His disciples the benefits of His atonement."—*Early Writings,* p. 260.

It becomes obvious that the two pillars of the atonement are the cross and the resurrection. It was Jesus, dying and living again, who made possible the salvation of mankind. A look at the experiences of Jesus may help us to understand what we mean when we say "I accept the death of Jesus Christ on Calvary as the atoning sacrifice for the sins of men."

Jesus looked forward to the cross as a self-imposed obligation. He knew that there was a cross at the end of His earthly journey, and He knew that the cross would be followed by resurrection. He shared this knowledge with His disciples: "From that time forth began Jesus to shew unto his disciples, how that he must go unto Jerusalem, and suffer many things of the elders and the chief priests and scribes, and be killed, and be raised again the third day" (Matt. 16:21).

In the Garden of Gethsemane, Jesus said, " 'Now is my soul troubled. And what shall I say? "Father, save me from this hour?" No, for this purpose I have come to this hour. Father, glorify thy name' " (John 12:27, 28, R.S.V.).

These texts, and similar ones, picture a Saviour who had chosen the way of the cross because love demanded that He make the supreme sacrifice for the salvation of man. Many Christians have lived under the shadow of the fear of martyrdom, but for Jesus martyrdom was certain. He "must" suffer. Love had no alternative.

Jesus anticipated that His death would provide unique benefits for His followers. These benefits were to be much greater than mere example or encouragement. He declared that He came "to give his life a ransom for many" (Mark 10:45). The word *ransom* refers to the price of release or redemption. What Jesus meant is made very clear in 1 Peter 1:18-21: "You know that you were ransomed from the futile ways inherited from your fathers, not with perishable things such as silver or gold, but with the precious blood of Christ. . . . Through him you have confidence in God, who raised him from the dead and gave him glory, so that your faith and hope are in God" (R.S.V.).

At His last supper with His disciples, Jesus described in a very graphic way the unique benefits of His death to His followers. He designated the bread as a symbol of His body, and the wine as a symbol of His blood. And He said

GOOD NEWS FROM CALVARY / 23

His body was broken "for you" and His blood was shed "for you."

Jesus had no question as to the benefits of His sacrifice. His incarnation, life, suffering, death—and His resurrection—were all part of the way in which salvation was made available for mankind.

Jesus shrank from the cross. He was no psychotic, plunging into persecution to satisfy unfulfilled urges or frustrated dreams. He was sensitive to suffering, and was particularly sensitive to the sin that caused suffering. In Gethsemane, He prayed, "O my Father, if it be possible, let this cup pass from me" (Matt. 26:39).

Jesus' death was unique in that He never reached a point of no return. He had the power at any point to have "rung the bell" on Caiaphas, on Pilate, on Herod, on the soldiers who nailed Him to the cross. He told His listeners, "Therefore doth my Father love me, because I lay down my life, that I might take it again. No man taketh it from me, but I lay it down of myself. I have power to lay it down, and I have power to take it again. This commandment have I received of my Father" (John 10:17, 18). Jesus refused to exercise His power. He was determined to fulfill His mission. This is part of what we mean by atonement. We can't fathom it, but we can thank God for a Saviour who willingly suffered and died in order that we might live.

The source of the atonement was divine love. God loved, Jesus loved, the Spirit loved. Jesus demonstrated His love on the cross. He asked the Father to forgive those who had nailed Him there. He provided for the care of His mother. He brought salvation to the penitent thief. In all of these things, He was expressing the perfect love that was necessary to accomplish man's redemption. When we say we accept the death of Jesus as an atoning sacrifice, we are accepting His matchless love.

To summarize what the Gospels have to say about Jesus' atoning sacrifice: Jesus was God revealed in the flesh in order to make salvation possible for man. This salvation could be realized only by an ultimate expression of love, so Jesus moved with firm steps to Calvary. He could have avoided the cross, but love said, No! Throughout the horrible experience of trial, degradation, scourging, crucifixion, He never lost His love or His dignity. For a brief time, He felt forsaken by His Father ("My God, my God, why hast thou forsaken me?" [Matt. 27:46]). But He died with words of fulfillment on His lips ("It is finished" [John 19:30]).

This was the atonement. When He offered Himself on the cross He atoned for the sins of mankind. Christians have tried to describe what happened on that dark Friday. Jim Bishop, author of *The Day Christ Died,* describes the atonement as follows:

"It was victory beyond their most exalted imaginings. He had come here to die. And He had died. He had come to preach a new covenant with His Father, and He had preached it. He had come to tell man that the way to everlasting life was love—love for the other, love for Him, and His love for all—and He had proved this by laying down His life in a torrent of torment—for them."—Page 347.

The apostle Paul rose to heights of eloquence in his description of the atonement: "While we were yet helpless, at the right time Christ died for the ungodly. Why, one will hardly die for a righteous man—though perhaps for a good man one will dare even to die. But God shows his love for us in that while we were yet sinners Christ died for us" (Rom. 5:6-8, R.S.V.).

Seventh-day Adventist author Ellen White describes

the atonement as follows: "Christ was treated as we deserve, that we might be treated as He deserves. He was condemned for our sins, in which He had no share, that we might be justified by His righteousness, in which we had no share. He suffered the death which was ours, that we might receive the life which was His. 'With His stripes we are healed.'"—*The Desire of Ages,* p. 25.

Jesus' atonement on the cross was the fulfillment of a prophecy made centuries before, and recorded in Isaiah 52 and 53. Notice how graphically the prophet predicts the cross:

"Surely he has borne our griefs
    and carried our sorrows;
yet we esteemed him stricken,
    smitten by God, and afflicted.
But he was wounded for our transgressions,
    he was bruised for our iniquities;
upon him was the chastisement that made us whole,
    and with his stripes we are healed.
All we like sheep have gone astray;
    we have turned every one to his own way;
and the Lord has laid on him
   the iniquity of us all" (Isa. 53:4-6, R.S.V.).

The chapter closes with an unmistakable reference to atonement:

"Yet he bore the sin of many,
   and made intercession for the transgressors" (verse 12).

In the quotation from the *Seventh-day Adventist Encyclopedia* at the beginning of this chapter, it was stated that Jesus' present intercession in our behalf is part of the atonement. This idea has been misunderstood by some. They have asked, "Was not the atonement completed at the cross?" Yes, at the cross complete provision was made for man's salvation. But this gracious *provision* had to be followed by *appropriation.* A contemporary Seventh-day Adventist theologian has put it thus:

"The atonement as the objective work of Christ is God's provision for man's salvation. The experience of faith is man's appropriation of what God has provided. Had there been no provision, there could be no salvation. If the salvation be not appropriated, then the provision is as good as not having been made. God provides the way, but man must accept it. If a person does not accept it, then it is for that person as if the provision had never been made."—Edward Vick, *Let Me Assure You,* p. 45.

The idea that Jesus is now at work dispensing the benefits of the atonement is suggested by another contemporary Seventh-day Adventist theologian:

"The cross is the supreme act of God for man's redemption. But that is only one aspect of Christ's work toward the final at-one-ment. Reconciliation is effected by the living Christ. It is not something that happened two thousand years ago. At-one-ment is experienced only as men daily live a life of trust and dependence on Him. The ultimate redemption of all things unto Himself can never be achieved until man is won to a life of unwavering faith and obedience. It is the living Christ of the present who saves, redeems, reconciles."—Edward Heppenstall, *Our High Priest,* pp. 29, 30.

It is part of the gospel that the same Jesus who died on the cross to provide the atonement rose again and ministers in our behalf to make the atonement a reality to us. More will be said about this in a later chapter.

The article in the baptismal vow asks us to believe that "through faith in His shed blood men are saved from sin and its penalty." *"By grace are ye saved through faith"*

GOOD NEWS FROM CALVARY / 27

(Eph. 2:8) is the New Testament formula—*God's* grace and *our* faith. It was grace—undeserved love—that made the cross possible. It is faith—acceptance, trust, commitment—that makes the cross effective in our lives. Grace is God's hand reaching down to us. Faith is our hand reaching up to Him. And when God's hand of grace takes hold of our hand of faith, He "saves" us. This is what "salvation" is all about. In fact, it is what Christianity is all about. The dying Christ made the atonement for us, and the living Christ enables us to have the faith to accept it.

The meaning of the cross has sometimes been best described in the hymns of the Christian faith. Here is one of the finest:

There was One who was willing to die in my stead,
    That a soul so unworthy might live,
And the path to the cross He was willing to tread,
    All the sins of my life to forgive.

He is tender and loving and patient with me,
    While He cleanses my heart of its dross,
But 'there's no condemnation;' I know I am free,
    For my sins are all nailed to the cross.

I will cling to my Saviour and never depart—
    I will joyfully journey each day,
With a song on my lips and a song in my heart,
    That my sins have been taken away.

They are nailed to the cross, they are nailed to the cross,
    O how much He was willing to bear!
With what anguish and loss, Jesus went to the cross!
    But He carried my sins with Him there.—*Church Hymnal,* No. 123.

CHAPTER III

Good News About Salvation

"Renouncing the world and its sinful ways, have you accepted Jesus Christ as your personal Saviour, and do you believe that God, for Christ's sake, has forgiven your sin and given you a new heart?"

THIS ARTICLE in the baptismal certificate has four parts: (1) it assumes that the candidate for baptism has "renounced the world and its sinful ways"; (2) it asks that the candidate accept Jesus Christ as his *personal* Saviour; (3) it asks that the candidate believe that his sin has been forgiven; and (4) it asks that the candidate believe that God has given him a "new heart." These four important themes will be discussed under the headings "Renouncing the World," "A Personal Saviour," "Forgiveness of Sin," and "A New Heart."

Renouncing the World. What does this mean? Does it mean to renounce the people of the world as unworthy of our attention or consideration? This cannot be, for "God so loved the *world,* that he gave his only begotten Son..." Does it mean that Christians should separate themselves into ghettos and communes, and live within their own peculiar counterculture? This cannot be God's plan, for

He said to His followers, "Go ye therefore, and teach all nations . . ."

The real meaning of "renouncing the world" is found in Romans 12:2: "Don't let the world around you squeeze you into its mould, but let God re-make you so that your whole attitude of mind is changed" (Phillips). There are certain characteristics that mark the difference between "the world" and the followers of Jesus: The world puts self at the center. Christians give God the central place in their lives. The world is motivated by rivalry and distrust. Christians are motivated by good will to all mankind. The world puts great value on wealth and fame. The Christian accepts the Holy Scriptures as his norm. The world has no assurance of a life beyond the present. The Christian believes in life everlasting.

To "renounce the world" means to renounce the selfishness, the materialism, the paganism that characterize so much of the world's culture. The candidate for Christian baptism is asked to take seriously the counsel of John the apostle:

"Do not love the world or anything that belongs to the world. If you love the world, you do not love the Father. Everything that belongs to the world—what the sinful self desires, what people see and want, and everything in this world that people are so proud of—none of this comes from the Father; it all comes from the world. The world and everything in it that men desire is passing away; but he who does the will of God lives forever" (1 John 2:15-17, T.E.V.).

A Personal Saviour. In Chapter II we discussed Jesus as our Saviour. It is possible to believe that Jesus came to save the world or the church, but to overlook the great news that He came to save *me.* Jesus died for *me. My* salvation was made available to me on His resurrection morning. Jesus represents *me* in His Father's presence today. Jesus hears *my* prayers. He guides *my* life. He is concerned when *I* suffer. He rejoices in *my* victories. He is coming again for *me*.

The person who is planning to be baptized into the Seventh-day Adventist faith should ask himself certain questions: Why am I making this decision? Is it because of my upbringing? Is it because of the influence of friends? Is it fear? Is it the result of a reasoned, intellectual decision? Or am I seeking a deep, personal identification with Jesus as a *personal* Saviour? Am I anxious to learn the joy of communion with God in prayer? Am I seeking divine guidance in my decisions, in my thinking, in my actions, in my words, in my influence?

The Bible speaks of this experience as "knowing God." John said it well: " 'And this is eternal life, that they [all Christians] know thee the only true God, and Jesus Christ whom thou hast sent'" (John 17:3, R.S.V.).

The psalmist caught the idea of a personal relationship with God. On one occasion, when he was under great stress, he made a statement that can be of help to believers, new and old. He said, "I lie awake at night thinking of you—of how much you have helped me—and how I rejoice through the night beneath the protecting shadow of your wings. I follow close behind you, protected by your strong arm" (Ps. 63:6-8, T.L.B.).

In Christ, God was with the fishermen in their boats, the beggars by the roadside, the guests at a wedding. In Christ, He associated with publicans at their feasts, with mourners at a funeral, with children at their play. He was the companion of worshipers at the synagogue and at the Temple, and of carpenters at Nazareth. God's unfathomable grace caused Him not only to pay a great price for man's redemption but also to identify Himself with man as his companion and friend.

A classic statement from Adventist literature summarizes well the idea of a personal relationship with a personal Saviour and a personal God: " 'Do you ask why I believe in Jesus? Because He is to me a divine Saviour. Why do I believe the Bible? Because I have found it to be the voice of God to my soul.' We may have the witness in ourselves that the Bible is true, that Christ is the Son of God."—*Steps to Christ*, p. 112.

Happy is the new convert who finds this experience at the beginning of his Christian walk and who maintains it and enjoys its growth throughout his entire life.

Forgiveness of Sin. "Not far from New York there is a cemetery where there is a grave which has inscribed upon its headstone just one word—'Forgiven.' There is no name, no date of birth or death. The stone is unembellished by the sculptor's art. There is no epitaph, no fulsome eulogy—just that one word, 'Forgiven.' But that is the greatest thing that can be said of any man, or written upon his grave, 'Forgiven.' "—*McCartney's Illustrations,* p. 132.

One of the fundamental concepts of the Christian faith is the belief that man stands in continual need of divine forgiveness. The prayer that Jesus taught His disciples included a petition for forgiveness. Christian liturgy from that day to this has included prayers for the forgiveness of sins. But all too often these prayers have been repeated lightly, with little appreciation of their meaning.

Many seem to believe that a hastily mumbled prayer for forgiveness at reasonably frequent intervals will take care of the sin problem. Others depend on confession into the ear of a priest or of a psychiatrist. Guilt is a common human problem that different people try to solve in different ways.

To the Christian, forgiveness is one of the manifestations of God's grace. "If we confess our sins, he is faithful and just to forgive us our sins." But the text does not stop here. It adds, "and to cleanse us from all unrighteousness" (1 John 1:9). Forgiveness is not a means of tolerating sin, but of curing it.

It is not a light thing for God to forgive sin, because He sees it in all its hideousness. God cannot condone wrongdoing, but He loves the wrongdoer. Forgiveness, brought about by the infinite cost of the cross, is the ultimate proof of God's love. Nothing could be more unlike God than to tolerate sin, but nothing is more like God than to forgive the sinner. One of the greatest blessings of becoming a Christian is that the load of guilt is taken away, and one of the blessings of being a Christian is that, through God's forgiving grace, that burden of guilt need never oppress us again.

Early in His ministry, Jesus gave His disciples what we know as the Lord's Prayer. In this prayer was the petition "Forgive us our trespasses." But these words are followed by the phrase "as we forgive those who trespass against us." Following the prayer, the Master added an explanatory comment: "For if ye forgive men their trespasses, your heavenly Father will also forgive you; but if ye forgive not men their trespasses, neither will your Father forgive your trespasses."

Near the middle of Jesus' ministry, He told a story illustrating this condition of forgiveness. A man owed his king "ten thousand talents," but the king forgave him his huge debt. The same man insisted on collecting from a fellow servant who owed him only "an hundred pence." The king's wrath was severe. The lesson is spelled out in Matthew 18:35: "So likewise shall my heavenly Father do also unto you, if ye from your hearts forgive not every one

GOOD NEWS ABOUT SALVATION / 33

his brother their trespasses."

During the final week before His crucifixion, Jesus said, "And when ye stand praying, forgive, if ye have ought against any: that your Father also which is in heaven may forgive you your trespasses" (Mark 11:25). And later, during the same tragic week, He illustrated what He meant. Hanging on the cross, He prayed, "Father, forgive them" (Luke 23:34). To whom did He refer? This prayer was a sincere petition in behalf of Judas, who betrayed Him; of the Pharisees and priests, who hated Him so violently; of Pilate and Herod, who could have delivered Him; of the hardened soldiers, who tortured Him; and of all mankind, who helped place Him on the cross. Jesus, who needed no forgiveness, was willing to forgive.

These excerpts from the teaching and example of Jesus tell us something that evangelical theology has sometimes overlooked. In a worthy endeavor to extol the love and grace of God, it is sometimes stated that man's sins were completely atoned for—all forgiven—at the cross, that there are no conditions for salvation. Redemption, they insist, is free: "Jesus paid it all." These statements are true, properly understood; but Jesus makes it plain that *if we are to receive the most basic blessing of the gospel—forgiveness—we must be willing to forgive.*

Paul's teaching is the same: "Be ye kind one to another, tenderhearted, forgiving one another, even as God for Christ's sake hath forgiven you" (Eph. 4:32). Man is saved by God's grace through faith. He is not saved by his works. Yet the statement of the Saviour Himself must not be forgotten: "If ye forgive not men their trespasses, neither will your Father forgive your trespasses" (Matt. 6:15). A penitent sinner must recognize his responsibility to his fellowmen in order to secure forgiveness, without which salvation is not possible.

This doctrine has an intensely practical significance. It is easy to repeat the words in church "Forgive us our trespasses," but the real test comes in the realm of human relationships. Suppose someone cheats *me* out of everything I own. Suppose someone lies about *me.* Suppose someone harms *my* child. In circumstances like these, *can I forgive?*

The cross of Christ demonstrates for all time that forgiveness cannot be taken lightly. Jesus paid an infinite price that He might forgive. In so doing, He gave His followers an example of forgiving love that has spoken to the hearts of men and women throughout the ages. From Calvary comes the message that God's children may be forgiven and must be forgiving. This is one of the basic doctrines of the Christian faith.

The new covenant—the covenant of grace—is predicted in the Old Testament. The Lord said to the prophet Jeremiah, "I will put my law in their inward parts, and write it in their hearts; and will be their God, and they shall be my people. . . . I will forgive their iniquity, and I will remember their sin no more" (Jer. 31:33, 34). Forgiveness brings freedom. There will be no more sleepless nights spent regretting sins that have been forgiven. There will be no more fear and insecurity regarding my relationship to God and my hope of salvation. By the same token, there will be no more resentment against those who have wronged me! It is all part of the same package.

When a person takes his baptismal vows, he is asked to "believe" that the Lord, who promised to forgive, has actually forgiven. This can be the door to freedom, to happiness, to security, to hope. It is not necessary for us to suffer torment because of our sins, or try to expiate for our sins, when God has promised to forgive them if we will

GOOD NEWS ABOUT SALVATION / 35

only believe Him, commit ourselves to Him, and forgive our fellow men. Amazing grace! Good news indeed!

A New Heart. In his book *What Is a Christian?* Leonard Griffith tells of the conversion of Tolstoi. He quotes Tolstoi's testimony:

"Five years ago I came to believe in Christ and my life suddenly changed. I ceased to desire what I had previously desired and began to desire what I formerly did not want. What previously seemed good to me seemed evil, and what seemed evil seemed good. It happened to me as it happens to a man who goes out on some business and on the way suddenly decides that the business is unnecessary and returns home. All that was on his right is now on his left, and all that was on his left is now on his right. The former wish—to get as far as possible from home—has changed into a wish to be as near as possible to it. The direction of my life and my desires became different, and good and evil changed places."—Page 41.

This is one way of describing what is meant by "a new heart." The new birth is followed by a new life. "God, who began this good work in you, will carry it on until it is finished in the Day of Christ Jesus" (Phil. 1:6, T.E.V.). "So get rid of your old self. . . . Your hearts and minds must be made completely new, and you must put on the new self, which is created in God's likeness and reveals itself in the true life that is upright and holy" (Eph. 4:22-24, T.E.V.). "The Spirit has given us life; he must also control our lives" (Gal. 5:25, T.E.V.). "It was not because of any good works that we ourselves had done, but because of his own mercy that he saved us, through the Holy Spirit, who gives us new birth and new life by washing us" (Titus 3:5, T.E.V.).

The "new heart," or new life, whichever way we want to say it, will make a difference. Our homes will be improved. We shall be happier and more effective in our vocations. We shall be more sensitive to human need. We shall be honest in a dishonest world. We shall be decent in a dirty world. We shall be generous in a greedy world. We shall be kind in a harsh world. We shall be tolerant in an intolerant world. We shall find peace in a troubled world. All of these improvements will result from the "new heart" that God gives us in response to our faith.

This article in the baptismal vow asks the new believer to "renounce," "accept," "believe"—renounce the "world," accept Jesus as a personal Saviour, believe that he is forgiven and transformed. Truly experienced, it is the beginning of a new life—a life that will reach its fullness in the heavenly kingdom. It can be the most unforgettable experience of a lifetime. Such a vow should be like the Great Divide of a mountain range. Everything is different. There is a new reason for living. There is a new nature, a new Lord, new motivations, and a new hope. "When anyone is joined to Christ, he is a new being; the old is gone, the new has come" (2 Cor. 5:17, T.E.V.).

CHAPTER IV

Good News About Our Friend in Heaven

"Do you accept by faith the righteousness of Christ, recognizing Him as your Intercessor in the heavenly sanctuary, and do you claim His promise to strengthen you by His indwelling Spirit, so that you may receive power to do His will?"

THIS IS an exceedingly important article in the baptismal vow. Rightly understood and warmly accepted, it can make the difference between humdrum conformity and a life of happiness, growth, security, and hope. Let us examine this article phrase by phrase:

"Do you accept by faith the righteousness of Christ?" Is this a mere theological cliché, or does it describe a significant and attainable experience? Let us explore how salvation works:

First, man's salvation has its origin in the grace of God. Grace is God's love for people who don't deserve love. God, in His amazing grace, decided to make provision for the salvation of mankind. The Father, the Son, and the Holy Spirit combined their resources to provide a plan by which man could be rescued from his lostness and transformed into a child of God.

This salvation is the result of the righteousness (rightness) of Jesus being credited to us in place of our unrighteousness (wrongness). This happens when we become Christians. We are accepted as if we had never sinned. After we become Christians, the same divine "rightness" is imparted (given) to us as we are ready to accept it, and we grow more and more like our Lord.

Why do some people experience this rescue and transformation, while many others do not? The answer is *faith*. "By grace [God's] are ye saved through faith [yours]" (Eph. 2:8). God is willing to rescue and transform everyone, but only a few respond to His grace. Faith is responding to God's grace by *believing, accepting, making a firm commitment to Him.* As we have said before, grace is the hand of God reaching down to save us. Faith is our hand reaching up toward Him. Salvation is God grasping our uplifted hand and lifting us out of our sin and despair into a life under His protection and guidance.

This does not mean that we become sinless saints when we become Christians. It does mean that our sins are forgiven, we are "born again," and under God's guidance we grow "to mature manhood, to the measure of the stature of the fulness of Christ" (chap. 4:13, R.S.V.). This process of growth continues as long as life lasts, or until our Saviour returns.

This great salvation becomes ours when we "accept by faith the righteousness of Christ." And God will never repudiate us as along as we do not forsake our faith in Him. He is patient with our weaknesses and willing to forgive our failures. He will hold on to us as long as we don't wriggle out of His grasp. God has never promised "once saved, always saved," but He has assured us, "once saved, very much saved."

"Recognizing Him as your Intercessor in the heavenly

sanctuary." What is Jesus doing *now?* The answer comes from God's Word, positive and clear: "When he [Jesus] had made purification for sins, he sat down at the right hand of the Majesty on high." "Since then we have a great high priest who has passed through the heavens, Jesus, the Son of God, let us hold fast our confession. For we have not a high priest who is unable to sympathize with our weaknesses, but one who in every respect has been tempted as we are, yet without sinning. Let us then with confidence draw near to the throne of grace, that we may receive mercy and find grace to help in time of need" (Heb. 1:3; 4:14-16, R.S.V.). He is our Friend in heaven.

This text used the example of the Old Testament priesthood in which a priest approached God on behalf of the people. The Epistle to the Hebrews tells us we no longer need a *human* priest, for Jesus intercedes directly in our behalf. The gospel of Jesus Christ involves more than His life and death here on earth. It includes also what He has been doing in heaven from the time of His ascension until now. He has been applying the benefits of His atoning sacrifice to each one who comes to Him in faith.

Do we feel weak and needy? Are we tempted and tested? Do we have problems, worries, fears, and tensions? Have we tangled the threads of life? Do we stagger under a burden of guilt? We have a living Jesus who is on twenty-four-hour duty. He is ready to help us, and He will never turn us away. He is our Friend in heaven.

We can have complete confidence in the loving concern of Jesus. He says, " 'Him who comes to me I will not cast out' " (John 6:37, R.S.V.). Jesus' ministry for us now is as important a part of the plan of salvation as was His death on the cross. What He began on the cross, He is continuing in the heavenly sanctuary and will complete when He comes again.

There is security in the living Christ. Paul wrote, "For I know whom I have believed, and am persuaded that he is able to keep that which I have committed unto him against that day" (2 Tim. 1:12). The risen Jesus, the One who intercedes for us in heaven, is just as real as He was when He appeared to Mary Magdalene at the tomb or to the two disciples on the way to Emmaus, or to Peter at the seashore. He is just as concerned about His followers as when He dried Mary's tears, dispelled the disciples' fears, dissolved Thomas' doubts, and forgave Peter's disloyalty. Since He is not now limited by space or time, He is able to meet the needs of everyone, everywhere. He is our Friend in heaven.

The term *intercession* has often been misunderstood. Some people picture God as eager to judge, punish, and destroy; but they picture Jesus as interceding with His Father to be merciful.

The Greek word translated "intercede" has been defined as meaning "to meet with in order to converse" (George Abbott-Smith, *A Manual Greek Lexicon of the New Testament,* p. 157). Jesus is not saying to His Father, "Won't You please save these people?" but "What can We do to help them?" Jesus is not prodding an unwilling Father, but collaborating with a concerned and loving Father. They both are our Friends in heaven. The following quotation states this interpretation very clearly:

"Jehovah did not deem the plan of salvation complete while invested only with His love. He has placed at His altar an Advocate clothed in His nature. As our intercessor, Christ's office work is to introduce us to God as His sons and daughters. He intercedes in behalf of those who receive Him. With His own blood He has paid their ransom. By virtue of His own merits He gives them power to become members of the royal family, children of the heavenly King. And the Father demonstrates His infinite love for Christ by receiving and welcoming Christ's friends as His friends."—*Counsels to Parents and Teachers,* p. 14.

This doesn't sound like the language of a law court. It sounds rather like a joyful family reunion, with God welcoming as friends those who follow Christ. The Holy Trinity work as one in the salvation of man—God, our Father; Jesus, our Representative; the Holy Spirit, our Helper. What more could be done to make possible our salvation?

"Do you claim His promise to strengthen you by His indwelling Spirit?"

The idea of the "indwelling Spirit" is a theme of the apostle Paul. To the Romans he wrote: "But you are not in the flesh, you are in the Spirit, if the Spirit of God really dwells in you. Any one who does not have the Spirit of Christ does not belong to him. But if Christ be in you, although your bodies are dead because of sin, your spirits are alive because of righteousness. If the Spirit of him who raised Jesus from the dead dwells in you, he who raised Christ Jesus from the dead will give life to your mortal bodies also through his Spirit which dwells in you" (Rom. 8:9-11, R.S.V.).

To the Corinthians, Paul wrote: "Do you not know that you are God's temple and that God's Spirit dwells in you? If any one destroys God's temple, God will destroy him. For God's temple is holy, and that temple you are" (1 Cor. 3:16, 17, R.S.V.). "Do you not know that your body is a temple of the Holy Spirit within you, which you have from God?" (chap. 6:19, R.S.V.).

What does it mean to have the Spirit dwelling within? A simple illustration may help us to understand. Consider the difference between a trailer and a truck. If a trailer is to get anywhere, it must be pulled, pushed, or carried. A truck has its source of power within. A "Christian" without the indwelling Spirit may have to be frightened, bribed, or coerced before he will pray, study his Bible, worship, obey his Lord, or perform his Christian duties. The Christian with the Spirit dwelling within is impelled by an inner motive to commit his life to the worship and service of God.

The indwelling Spirit contributes in many ways to our Christian lives. A few of them are:

1. He aids in our understanding of the Scriptures.
2. He interprets the gospel so we can understand it.
3. He imparts new life.
4. He assists us in our battle with temptation.
5. He enables us to distinguish truth from error.
6. He brings "the fruits of the Spirit" into our lives.
7. He imparts "the gifts of the Spirit" as He sees fit.
8. He reproves us when we are wayward.
9. He gives us good judgment and common sense.
10. He helps us in maintaining a Christian home.
11. He gives more than human strength when we need it.
12. He helps us cope with pain and adversity.
13. He helps us minister to the needs of others.
14. He enables us to reach worthwhile objectives.
15. He deepens our spiritual experience.

"The child of God is utterly dependent upon the Spirit for his spiritual birth, life, victory, and service. The Spirit lives within his heart. The more yielded he is to his indwelling Guest, the happier, healthier, holier, and more hopeful he becomes. This is the Christian's basic law of life. Would he experience daily the love and peace of the Saviour? Would he live on the highest spiritual plane? Would he have victory over temptation? Would he have a song in his soul? Would he be a blessing to others wherever he goes? Then he must keep yielded to the Spirit. Only then will his life and witness truly count for God."—Lindsell and Woodbridge, *op. cit.,* p. 66.

While we recognize the indwelling Spirit as our source of strength, we must not make the Spirit identical with our own spiritual experience. The Holy Spirit is a person—He is God. His presence within is a miracle of divine grace. His control of our thoughts, our emotions, our hopes, and our dreams is one of the "fringe benefits" of the gospel.

"So that you may receive power to do His will."

When did the early Christian church "receive power"? It was after the Holy Spirit came upon them. " 'But you shall receive power when the Holy Spirit has come upon you; and you shall be my witnesses in Jerusalem and in all Judea and Samaria and to the end of the earth' " (Acts 1:8, R.S.V.). Too often the church has sought power for its own sake. In the minds of too many, political and institutional influence has overshadowed the idea of power to do His will. Let us ask ourselves a very basic question: Are we really concerned about doing *His* will. Or are we trying to convince ourselves that *our* will is *His* will?

When we discuss doing God's will, we run the risk of being accused of legalism. But the legalist does not usually pray for God's Spirit to dwell within him so that he may do His will. The legalist tries to do His will in order that God's Spirit may dwell within him. There is a great difference.

One of the finest descriptions in Adventist literature of the transforming influence of the indwelling Spirit is found in the following quotation:

"Christ said to Nicodemus, 'The wind bloweth where it listeth, and thou hearest the sound thereof, but canst not tell whence it cometh, and whither it goeth: so is every one that is born of the Spirit.' Like the wind, which is invisible, yet the effects of which are plainly seen and felt, is the Spirit of God in its work upon the human heart. That regenerating power, which no human eye can see, begets a new life in the soul; it creates a new being in the image of God. While the work of the Spirit is silent and imperceptible, its effects are manifest. If the heart has been renewed by the Spirit of God, the life will bear witness to the fact. While we cannot do anything to change our hearts or to bring ourselves into harmony with God; while we must not trust at all to ourselves or our good works, our lives will reveal whether the grace of God is dwelling within us. A change will be seen in the character, the habits, the pursuits. The contrast will be clear and decided between what they have been and what they are. The character is revealed, not by occasional good deeds and occasional misdeeds, but by the tendency of the habitual words and acts. . . .

"Those who become new creatures in Christ Jesus will bring forth the fruits of the Spirit, 'love, joy, peace, long-suffering, gentleness, goodness, faith, meekness, temperance.' They will no longer fashion themselves according to the former lusts, but by the faith of the Son of God they will follow in His steps, reflect His character, and purify themselves even as He is pure. The things they once hated they now love, and the things they once loved they hate. The proud and self-assertive become meek and lowly in heart. The vain and supercilious become serious and unobtrusive. The drunken become sober, and the profligate pure."—*Steps to Christ,* pp. 57, 58.

This is not legalism. This is a statement of the way the gospel of Christ transforms the person who, energized by the Holy Spirit, responds in faith. "If any man be in Christ, he is a new creature" (2 Cor. 5:17). Christ, our Friend in heaven, makes possible this glorious transformation.

CHAPTER V

Good News About the Bible

"Do you believe that the Bible is God's inspired word, and that it constitutes the only rule of faith and practice for the Christian?"

THE CHRISTIAN world has been shaken by a prolonged and heated argument over the nature and authority of the Bible. There are many who believe that the Bible is merely a record of what certain men believed about God and of incidents in their lives.

There are many other Christians who believe that the Bible is a record of God's revelation to man. According to this viewpoint, the Bible writers were chosen of God to convey certain messages that He wanted people to hear. This viewpoint is reflected in Paul's counsel to Timothy:

"But as for you, continue in what you have learned and have become convinced of, because you know those from whom you learned it, and how from infancy you have known the holy Scriptures, which are able to make you wise for salvation through faith in Christ Jesus. All Scripture is God-breathed and is useful for teaching, rebuking, correcting and training in righteousness, so that the man of God may be thoroughly equipped for every good work" (2 Tim. 3:14-17, N.I.V.).

It is obvious that article five in the Seventh-day Adventist baptismal vow espouses the position that the Bible is "God's inspired word," and that it "constitutes the only rule of faith and practice for the Christian." Seventh-day Adventists place great stress on the Bible. But even conservative Christians have sometimes misused and misinterpreted the Bible.

What are some of the principles that should guide us as we relate ourselves to the Word of God?

First, let us note a few warnings:

The Bible is not a book of magic. Normally, Christians do not receive divine guidance by opening it at random and reading the first text that meets their eyes. The Bible is a book to be read thoughtfully and prayerfully.

Neither is the Bible a book of rules intended to meet every circumstance of life with computerlike precision. It is not a blueprint, but a book of general principles that can guide us in life's decisions and commitments. The Bible does not tell us how to compute our income tax, but if we listen to its teaching, we will do our computation honestly.

The Bible is not a word-for-word transcription of the mind of God. God chose to reveal His will through men. The writers of the Bible were "His penmen, not His pen." He seldom dictated what they should write, but He filled their minds with revelations, insights, and understanding which they relayed in their own words and style.

Neither is the study of the Bible a substitute for the study of science, history, literature, and other areas of learning. For example, one can learn much about health in the Bible, but it takes more than the study of the Bible to make a physician.

The study of the Bible is not free from problems. It was written in ancient languages in the context of cultures that have long since disappeared. All the original manuscripts have been lost, and generations of translators and copyists have left their mark on its pages. But despite the problems of versions, translations, and differing texts, the Bible is adequate to communicate the will of God to man. God has preserved for us all the "good news" we need for salvation. Like a great ship, battered and scarred by many voyages and severe storms, it is still able to carry its passengers to their destinations.

What are the legitimate purposes of the Bible for modern man?

First and foremost, the Bible reveals the Christian good news. It reveals God's activities in man's behalf, including the Incarnation, the cross, the resurrection and Christ's priestly intercession. It is more than a history of the affairs of men; it is a revelation of the purposes of God.

Second, it brings comfort and strength in times of stress, discouragement, and pain. The Bible is an "upbeat" book, full of encouragement and hope.

Third, it reveals to man—in broad outline—how he should live and relate to his fellow men. It gives him an objective foundation on which can be built an understanding of right and wrong.

Fourth, the Bible gives insight into the future, both for the duration of the present world and into the world to come. It consistently reminds its readers that the gospel will have a consummation, the second coming of our Lord. Resurrection is one of the themes of God's Word.

The late G. Ernest Wright, prominent archeologist and Biblical scholar, has said it well: "Christianity has always held that the Bible is a very special book unlike any other book in the world. It is the most important of all books because in it, and in it alone, the true God has made

Himself known to man with clarity. The world is full of sacred literatures and it is full of gods. But in the vast confusion the one source which can be relied upon for the truth is the Bible. There we are told about the events which brought the church into being, and the purpose for its being. There we encounter the answer to the meaning of our own lives and of the history in which we live. There the frightening gulf between our weak, ignorant, and mortal lives and the infinity of power and space in our universe is really bridged. There we discover our deity defined and our God revealed."—*The Book of the Acts of God,* p. 15.

It is important to recognize the Bible as the Word of God, but it is equally necessary to learn to love and enjoy it. Many moderns have not grown up with the Bible. Its language is unfamiliar, formidable, difficult. Others have been so thoroughly exposed to the Bible that it seems like "old stuff"; it has lost its appeal through overfamiliarity. In other words, one person may not enjoy reading the Bible because it is unfamiliar. Another may resent the Book because it is too familiar.

May I make a few suggestions intended to help the modern person in his endeavor to appreciate and understand the Bible:

Don't begin by trying to read the Bible through, "from cover to cover," like a book you might borrow from a library. It is really a collection of sixty-six books, written over a period of many centuries by many different writers. The Bible is different.

The central theme of the Book is the salvation of man, and the main character is Jesus Christ. The story of His life and teaching is found in the four Gospels—Matthew, Mark, Luke, and John. The shortest and probably the first Gospel to be written is Mark's. Why not try reading it first?

It has only sixteen chapters—about as long as a full-length magazine article. If possible, read this book at one sitting, or, at the most, during two or three sittings.

When you have finished a thoughtful reading of Mark, you will have been introduced, or reintroduced, to Jesus. You will have felt the impact of His life and teaching, and you will have seen the plan of salvation as centered in the cross and the resurrection. And you can hardly help enjoying Mark. He is easy to read and understand.

I can hear someone saying, "Wait a minute! It isn't easy for me. The book is full of thees and thous—unfamiliar words and phrases." Perhaps you have been reading the King James Version, translated into English in 1611. The language is that of the seventeenth century. If this gives you problems, try the Revised Standard Version, *The New English Bible,* or *The New International Version.* If English is a second language for you, try the American Bible Society's *Today's English Version,* known as the *Good News Bible.* Remember that paraphrases do not always follow the original languages as closely as do the more traditional versions. Whichever translation you choose, it is important that you understand what you are reading.

When you have finished Mark, I would suggest that you read the Acts of the Apostles. This thrilling story of the early church was written by Luke the physician, also author of the third Gospel. Acts gives an insight into the great characters who pioneered the Christian faith. You will come to know Peter and Paul and the other characters as you follow them through the fascinating chapters of this book. And you will *never* get bored! You will enjoy the suspense of stories of imprisonment, travel, shipwreck, and conquest. You will no doubt find yourself wanting to identify more closely with the Christian faith as you witness the stature of the men and women who pioneered for Christ.

After you have finished Mark and Acts, there are several directions your reading may take. You might do well at this time to turn back to the Old Testament and acquaint yourself with the backgrounds of the Bible. You may want to read Genesis and Exodus to review God's dealings with men up to the giving of the Ten Commandments on Mount Sinai. You may find yourself so intrigued by the Old Testament narratives that you will continue through Joshua, Judges, Samuel, Kings, and Chronicles. You will find sections in these books that you may wish to scan. On the other hand, you will find scores of fascinating personalities and incidents that portray the dealings of God with man.

As you read these Old Testament stories, you will be impressed with the human weaknesses of many of the characters. You will also be impressed with God's patience. God uses the best people He can find in every generation, but many of them have serious shortcomings.

Now it may be time for you to return to the New Testament. You may wish to read the other three Gospels. There is a wonderful group of letters known as the Epistles. Most of these were written by Paul; others were penned by Peter, James, John, and Jude. Some of these letters are difficult theological treatises—such as parts of Romans and Galatians. Feel your way! You possibly will not want to start with Romans, even though it is the first of the Epistles in our Bible. You might want to start with First and Second Thessalonians or Philippians or First Corinthians. As in swimming, don't venture too far beyond your depth until you can at least float!

You will notice that the final chapters of most of the Epistles deal with practical Christian living. For example,

GOOD NEWS ABOUT THE BIBLE / 51

the twelfth through the sixteenth chapters of Romans are entirely different from chapters one through eleven.

There is another type of Old Testament book you may enjoy. I refer to the poetry and "wisdom literature." Take some samplings of the Psalms, of Proverbs, of Job, of Ecclesiastes. Try reading them in a translation like *Today's English Version*. You will be fascinated with what you find.

Then there are the prophets. They are probably the most difficult books because the reader needs some understanding of the circumstances under which they were written. Try reading the first seven chapters of Daniel, the book of Jonah, selected chapters from Isaiah, and such books as Amos and Micah. You may need the help of a commentary at times. Again, go as far as you can.

The Letter to the Hebrews should not be overlooked. It is the Epistle of "better" things: A better priesthood, a better covenant, a better sacrifice, and a better faith. It shows the superiority of the gospel of Christ over the Hebrew experience and worship that preceded it.

And don't forget Revelation! Some parts of the book are puzzling. The key to understanding it is that it is a revelation of *Jesus Christ*. He is presented by the symbol of "the Lamb." More than twenty times this symbol is repeated. The book is of special importance as we approach the consummation of the Christian gospel—the second coming of Jesus.

At this point, I want to make sure that I am not misunderstood. I have advised the inexperienced reader of the Bible to read the Gospels, the book of Acts, some Old Testament narratives, some Old Testament poetry, some New Testament Epistles, and some Old and New Testament prophecies. I do not mean to imply that the entire Bible should not be read. I am assuming that the reading of the Bible in some such order as I have suggested will inspire many readers to read *all* the Epistles, *all* the prophets, and *all* the rest of the Sacred Book. Then, with this growing understanding of the Bible, you may choose to begin with Genesis and read through Revelation.

One doesn't learn to pilot an airplane by starting on a transoceanic flight. Neither does one learn to enjoy the Bible by beginning with the Lamentations of Jeremiah! The more difficult parts of the Bible will become understandable in due time.

Our discussion thus far has been aimed to help us study the Bible in such a way that we can understand it—and we all recognize that we cannot enjoy the Book unless we understand it. There is another phase of Bible study we must not overlook. We must recognize the practical value of the Bible as a devotional book.

Daily Bible reading need not *always* follow a book-by-book sequence. There is a place for browsing. When you go to the supermarket, you do not inspect evey item on every shelf. You look about until you see what you need; then you place that item in your basket. The next time you visit the store, your needs may be entirely different.

So it is in studying the Bible. In the quiet of your own home, with a prayer in your heart, pick up your Bible and read wherever the Spirit leads you—perhaps a psalm, possibly a chapter from Paul, sometimes a portion of a Gospel. Read until you find what you need for the day. Repeat this procedure the next day, and the next, and the next. The well will never run dry! A text that may mean little to you today may be just what you need most tomorrow.

The most important value of Bible study, as we

mentioned early in this chapter, is the discovery of Christ and His way of salvation. Articles two, three, and four of the baptismal vow have told us a bit about how to be saved. The present article puts us in personal contact with the Bible, the primary source of information about salvation.

It is helpful for us to remember that the Bible is not just a book for theologians and scholars. The same Holy Spirit who inspired the writers of the Bible will stand beside the humblest reader of the Sacred Word and help him to learn what he needs to know.

Books and sermons come and go, but the Bible remains "the only rule of faith and practice for the Christian." Theologians may argue about the meaning of inspiration, revelation, infallibility, inerrancy, and many other topics. But the Bible has a practical mission. Rightly used, it tells us what God is like, it reveals Jesus as our Saviour and Lord, it acquaints us with our Helper, the Holy Spirit, it recounts the experiences of God's people through many centuries, it explains the way of salvation, it describes the Christian life style, and it provides solutions to the problems of each day. The three words that characterize the message of the Bible are faith, hope, and love—"and the greatest of these is love" (1 Cor. 13:13, T.E.V.).

CHAPTER VI

Good News From Sinai

"Do you accept the Ten Commandments as still binding upon Christians; and is it your purpose, by the power of the indwelling Christ, to keep this law, including the fourth commandment, which requires the observance of the seventh day of the week as the Sabbath of the Lord?"

WE HAVE examined the first five of the thirteen articles of the baptismal vow. The person who answers Yes to the five questions is able to make the following confession of faith:

"I believe in God the Father, in His Son Jesus Christ, and in the Holy Spirit."

"I accept the death of Jesus Christ on Calvary as the atoning sacrifice for the sins of men, and believe that through faith in His shed blood men are saved from sin and its penalty."

"I accept Christ as my personal Saviour. I believe that God has forgiven my sins and given me a new heart, and I renounce the world and its sinful ways."

"I accept by faith the righteousness of Christ, recognizing Him as my Intercessor in the heavenly sanctuary, and I claim His promise to strengthen me by His indwelling Spirit, so that I may receive power to do His will."

"I believe that the Bible is God's inspired word and that it constitutes the only rule of faith and practice for the Christian."

The key words in these five articles are *believe* and *accept*. I "believe" in the Holy Trinity; I "believe" that God forgives sins and saves from sin. I "believe" that the Bible is the Word of God. I "accept" Christ's death in my behalf; I "accept" Him as my personal Saviour; I "accept" the righteousness of Christ.

Thus far the new believer has stood in the presence of God with hands outstretched, palms up, accepting blessings that only God can give. This should have been one of the greatest experiences of his life. He has been introduced to God. He is no longer alone. He has been rescued and forgiven. He has been adopted by a heavenly Father. He has received God's Word as his guide.

I will never forget when I took this vow. It was June 9, 1923. My theological understanding was very immature, but I went home that day with a feeling of "belonging." I was eager and happy, looking forward to a life as a follower of Jesus. I have never forgotten the thrill of that memorable day in my life.

Article six of the baptismal vow is different. *The preceding articles have emphasized what Christ gives. Now we take a look at what He expects.* The Christian must not only accept the privileges of his faith—he must also accept the responsibilities. A contemporary evangelical author has said it well: "Christianity is no mere passive acquiescence in a series of propositions, however true. We may believe in the deity and salvation of Christ, and acknowledge ourselves to be sinners in need of his salvation; but this does not make us Christians. We have to make a personal response to Jesus Christ, committing ourselves unreservedly to him as our Saviour and Lord. . . .

"Jesus never concealed the fact that His religion included a demand as well as an offer. Indeed, the demand was as total as the offer was free. If He offered men His salvation, He also demanded their submission."—John R. W. Stott, *Basic Christianity,* p. 107.

Article six begins by referring to the Ten Commandments as "still binding upon Christians." Can this position be defended from the Bible? Let us look at a few texts:

On one occasion, an expert in Jewish law came to Jesus with a legal question. "Master," he asked, "which is the great commandent in the law?" Jesus answered, "Thou shalt love the Lord thy God with all thy heart, and with all thy soul, and with all thy mind. This is the first and great commandment. And the second is like unto it, Thou shalt love thy neighbour as thyself. On these two commandments hang all the law and the prophets" (Matt. 22:36-40).

How could one ask for a clearer reference to the Ten Commandments? The first four deal with our relationship to God; the last six with our relationship to people. In the Ten Commandments the principle of love is made relevant to the conditions and circumstances of man.

In the Sermon on the Mount, Jesus takes a positive stand in regard to law: "Think not that I am come to destroy the law, or the prophets: I am not come to destroy, but to fulfil. For verily I say unto you, Till heaven and earth pass, one jot or one tittle shall in no wise pass from the law, till all be fulfilled. Whosoever therefore shall break one of these least commandments, and shall teach men so, he shall be called the least in the kingdom of heaven: but whosoever shall do and teach them, the same shall be called great in the kingdom of heaven" (chap 5:17-19).

Jesus went on to explain how "law" should be interpreted. He said that the commandment that said "Thou shalt not kill" should be understood to include hate as well as murder. He enlarged the commandment "Thou shall not commit adultery" to include what today would be called "sexual fantasies." He even extended the command to love to include enemies as well as friends. His interpretation of the law included a love large enough to embrace all mankind.

The apostle Paul caught this idea. He said, "Owe no man any thing, but to love one another; for he that loveth another hath fulfilled the law. For this, Thou shalt not commit adultery, Thou shalt not kill, Thou shalt not steal, Thou shall not bear false witness, Thou shalt not covet; and if there be any other commandment, it is briefly comprehended in this saying, namely, Thou shalt love thy neighbor as thyself. Love worketh no ill to his neighbor: therefore love is the fulfilling of the law" (Rom. 13:8-10).

So we have ample New Testament evidence that the Ten Commandments, interpreted as ten ways of expressing love to God and other people, are still binding on Christians. This belief is shared by many evangelical Christians. All are agreed that law cannot save. Here is one very perceptive comment: "The law of God *enlightens* man concerning the nature and will of the Almighty; but it *does not empower* him for life's struggles. It *shows* him the way but it cannot *save* him. It *reveals* but it cannot *redeem*. It commands the sinner to fly but it provides no wings."—Lindsell and Woodbridge, *op. cit.,* p. 94. "The believer is indeed under grace. Yet the moral law has not been abrogated. On the contrary, it still reveals the attributes of God and His will for man; and it still brings sinners to their knees at the foot of Calvary. The convicting power of Sinai's thunders has not ceased."—*Ibid,* p. 97.

Article six of the baptismal vow is basically in harmony with evangelical theology. But there is one important difference: It declares that the ten-commandment law "requires the observance of the seventh day of the week as the Sabbath of the Lord." Evangelicals as a whole believe that the fourth command applies to Saturday in the Old Testament and Sunday in the New. As William Barclay has put it: "The Sabbath and Sunday are not the same. On the Sabbath the Jew remembers how God rested after the six days of Creation and on the Sunday the Christian remembers how Jesus rose from the dead."—*The Old Law and the New Law,* p. 23.

Before a person can say Yes to article six of the baptismal vow, he must believe that the Sabbath is the *only* day that can fulfill the obligation of the fourth commandment. The question is, Why not Sunday, or any other day? Why Sabbath? The following paragraphs suggest some answers to this crucial question:

First: No other day memorializes the creatorship of God.

Much modern theology disregards the importance of God as Creator, but the Bible is very clear on this point. It is also significant that the Bible names Jesus as the co-Creator.

"But to us there is but one God, the Father, *of whom are all things,* and we in him; and one Lord Jesus Christ, *by whom are all things,* and we by him" (1 Cor. 8:6).

"All things were made by him [Jesus]; and without him was not any thing made that was made" (John 1:3).

"To make all men see what is the fellowship of the mystery, which from the beginning of the world hath been hid in God, *who created all things by Jesus Christ*" (Eph. 3:9).

"Worship him that made heaven, and earth, and the sea, and the fountains of waters" (Rev. 14:7).

On every recurring Saturday, the Sabbathkeeper says to the world, "God and Christ created the universe, the world, and mankind." This is a basic truth that the world needs to remember, and God gave the Sabbath to man so that he might never forget his Maker. As long as the universe is filled with suns and galaxies and constellations; as long as the earth remains and our sun shines in the heavens; as long as there are times and seasons; as long as there are trees, flowers, and animals; as long as man lives—so long will the Sabbath be the divinely appointed symbol of a creating God.

It must be remembered that the Sabbath was designated and instituted by the Creator Himself. It was not man who decided to honor His Creator on that day; it was God who decreed that man should observe the day as a symbol of Creation. No decree or practice of man can alter the fact that Saturday, the seventh day of the week, is the Sabbath instituted by the Creator, the eternal memorial of the creatorship of God.

The second reason that no other day will do is the fact that the Sabbath is part of the government of God in the world. God told man how He wanted him to live, in the law given from Mount Sinai. A Seventh-day Adventist author has put it thus:

"The precepts of the Decalogue are adapted to all mankind, and they were given for the instruction and *government* of all. Ten precepts, brief, comprehensive, and authoritative, cover the duty of man to God and to his fellow man; and all are based upon the great fundamental principle of love. 'Thou shalt love the Lord thy God with all thy heart, and with all thy soul, and with all thy strength, and with all thy mind; and thy neighbour as thyself.' In the Ten Commandments these principles are carried out in detail, and made applicable to the condition and circumstances of man."—*Patriarchs and Prophets,* p. 305. (Italics supplied).

This law includes ten principles. Positively stated, they are as follows:

1. God must come first.
2. God must receive our exclusive worship.
3. God's name must be reverenced.
4. God's Sabbath must be observed.
5. Parents must be honored.
6. Life must be respected.
7. Purity must be preserved.
8. Property rights must be recognized.
9. Our neighbor's reputation must be protected.
10. Covetousness must be avoided.

It would seem reasonable to infer that as long as it is wrong to covet, to blast a neighbor's reputation, to steal, and to kill; as long as it is wrong to commit adultery, to ignore parents, to take God's name in vain, to worship idols, and to ignore God; *just so long it will be wrong to ignore God's Sabbath.* It is part of the package that was delivered personally to man by his Creator.

The third reason for the Sabbath's uniqueness is that the Bible describes it as a symbol of "rest" in Christ. This ties the seventh-day Sabbath to the Christian gospel. Where is this truth revealed?

In the Epistle to the Hebrews, the third chapter and the eleventh verse, God is quoted as saying, "So I sware in my wrath, They shall not enter into my rest." What was He talking about?

The context tells us He was describing the experience

of the Israelites in the wilderness on their way from Egypt to Canaan. They lived a hard, nomadic life, surrounded by danger, plagued by discomfort, and marked by insecurity. To them the Promised Land meant rest—home, rainfall, crops, and national identity.

Why did God decree that a whole generation of Israelites would not achieve their dream? The answer is found in chapter three, verses eighteen and nineteen: "And to whom sware he that they should not enter into his rest, but to them that *believed not?* so we see that they could not enter in because of *unbelief.*" It was a faithless generation that was denied the pleasures of rest in the Promised Land.

What does this mean to Christians? "Let *us* therefore fear, lest, a promise being left *us* of entering into his *rest,* any of you should seem to come short of it. For unto *us* was the gospel preached, as well as unto them: but the word preached did not profit them, not being mixed with *faith* in them that heard it. For *we* which have *believed* do enter into *rest*" (chap. 4:1-3).

The experience of Israel is here used as a type of Christian experience. The Christian's "rest" includes the forgiveness of his sins, his acceptance as a child of God, strength for Christian living, Christian security, and eventual eternal life. This "rest" is available through God's grace by faith. It is the great divine remedy for the meaninglessness of human life.

But the author of Hebrews does not stop here. In chapter four, verse four, he says, "For he spake in a certain place of the *seventh day* on this wise, And God did rest the seventh day from all his works." The Sabbath is presented as a symbol, both of the rest of Israel in the Promised Land and of the Christian's "rest" in Christ.

The identity of this symbol is made crystal clear in

verses eight through eleven:

"For if Jesus [R.S.V., "Joshua"] had given them rest, then would he [God] not afterward have spoken of another day. There remaineth therefore a rest to the people of God. For he that is entered into his rest, he also hath ceased from his own works, *as God did from his* [on the original Creation Sabbath]. Let us labour therefore to enter into that rest, lest any man fall after the same example of unbelief."

It must be remembered that the Sabbath memorializes not only a Creator at work but a Creator at rest: "And he rested on the seventh day" (Gen. 2:2). The Sabbath commemorated a finished work then, and it also commemorates a finished work now—the work of Jesus on the cross that entitles the person of faith to rest in Him.

This great symbol ties the Sabbath to the gospel. It is noteworthy that the letter to the Hebrew Christians, probably written during the seventh decade of the first century, did not introduce a new day of rest and worship. Rather, it told them that the day on which their ancestors had rested and worshiped for millenniums was a symbol of the rest provided by the Christ whom they now loved and served.

The fourth evidence of the fact that the Sabbath is the "one and only" day is the way in which it acts as a cohesive force, unifying and motivating Christians who observe it. Elton Trueblood in his book *Foundations of Reconstruction* has the following comment about the influence of the Sabbath in the history of ancient Judaism:

"When Judaism fell in 586 B.C. and the leaders, their temple having been wantonly destroyed, were taken to Babylon in captivity, their chance of survival was slight. The northern kingdoms had fallen more than a hundred years earlier and had never been revived. It has not been revived to this day. The southern kingdom would have gone the same way, and the whole of Western civilization would have been greatly impoverished thereby, if the prophet Ezekiel and others like him had not placed great emphasis upon the Sabbath. The Sabbath obvervance became an external badge which held people together as by a public witness. Once each week the people stood up to be counted in their alien environment and, though the weaklings naturally fell away, the faithful were consequently strengthened."—Page 42.

It is not always easy to be a Sabbathkeeper in the twentieth century. Sabbathkeepers have lost their employment because of their religious scruples. Sabbathkeepers in military service often meet a recurring crisis each weekend. Sabbathkeeping parents are faced with a heartbreaking dilemma in countries where school is held on Saturday.

Despite these and other problems, several million Sabbathkeepers throughout the world witness each week to their commitment to their Creator and Redeemer. No day of rest and worship based on human tradition could function as a badge, a cohesive force, a unifying principle. Sabbathkeepers are willing to suffer for their faith because they believe their Sabbath was ordained of God as a symbol of Creation and redemption.

If Seventh-day Adventism were to surrender the Bible Sabbath and simply call itself "Adventism," it would disintegrate rapidly. This falling apart would occur despite all the other good doctrines, excellent traditions, and praiseworthy activities of the church. The Sabbath is a "sign," a "badge," a "symbol," a "seal." It is not a means of salvation, but it is a flag unfurled by those who have experienced salvation. And Saturday is the only day that can qualify, for it is the only day with a divine origin and a tradition that spans the entire history of mankind.

Yes, good news broke through the smoke and thunders of Sinai. This good news was in the form of divine guidance as to how human beings should relate to God and to other human beings. God provided an authentic, reliable pattern of thought and conduct. The law in no way provided for forgiveness of transgressors, nor did it impart ability to live up to the standard. This was to be provided by the gospel. The law and the gospel were complementary to each other. One was diagnostic, the other remedial.

And the Sabbath of the law is as eternal as the law itself. It is still the symbol of "rest." It is still part of the government of God. It still memorializes God as Creator. And it is still a "sign" that makes a difference.

With credentials like these, no one need apologize for loyalty to the Ten Commandments, or the Sabbath of the fourth commandment. These institutions have revelation, history, and reason on their side. They span the centuries with a universal relevance that results from their divine origin. They will continue to bring depth and meaning into the experience of anyone who accepts them with faith and understanding.

CHAPTER VII

Good News About the Return of Jesus

"Is the soon coming of Jesus the blessed hope in your heart, and are you determined to be personally ready to meet the Lord, and to do all in your power to witness to His loving salvation, and by life and word to help others to be ready for His glorious appearing?"

PLEASE NOTICE that article seven of the baptismal vow is very personal. It does not say "Do you believe that Jesus is coming again?" but "Is the soon coming of Jesus the blessed hope in your heart?" Of course the Second Coming cannot be our "blessed hope" unless we believe it is going to happen, but it is possible to assent to the doctrine of Christ's return without it meaning much to us.

Let us take a brief look at what Jesus and His apostles said that justifies the existence of "Adventists"—believers in His second coming. Here are a few passages:

Jesus to His disciples at the Last Supper: " 'Let not your hearts be troubled; believe in God, believe also in me. In my Father's house are many rooms; if it were not so, would I have told you that I go to prepare a place for you? And when I go and prepare a place for you, I will come again and will take you to myself that where I am you may be also'" (John 14:1-3, R.S.V.).

At the ascension: "As they were looking on, he was lifted up, and a cloud took him out of their sight. And while they were gazing into heaven as he went, behold, two men stood by them in white robes, and said, 'Men of Galilee, why do you stand looking into heaven? This Jesus, who was taken up from you into heaven, will come in the same way as you saw him go into heaven'" (Acts 1:9-11, R.S.V.).

Paul's letter to Titus, pastor on the island of Crete: "For the grace of God has appeared for the salvation of all men, training us to renounce irreligion and worldly passions, and to live sober, upright, and godly lives in this world, awaiting our blessed hope, the appearing of the glory of our great God and Savior Jesus Christ, who gave himself for us to redeem us from all iniquity and to purify for himself a people of his own who are zealous for good deeds" (Titus 2:11-14, R.S.V.).

Instruction to Hebrew Christians: "He has appeared once for all at the end of the age to put away sin by the sacrifice of himself. And just as it is appointed for men to die once, and after that comes judgment, so Christ, having been offered once to bear the sins of many, will appear a second time, not to deal with sin but to save those who are eagerly waiting for him" (Heb. 9:26-28, R.S.V.).

Jesus to His disciples in His discourse on His return: "'But of that day and hour no one knows, not even the angels of heaven, nor the Son, but the Father only. . . . Watch therefore, for you do not know on what day your Lord is coming. . . . Therefore you also must be ready; for the Son of man is coming at an hour you do not expect" (Matt. 24:36-44, R.S.V.).

Paul to the Christians at Thessalonica: "For the Lord himself will descend from heaven with the archangel's call,

GOOD NEWS ABOUT THE RETURN OF JESUS / 67

and with the sound of the trumpet of God. And the dead in Christ will rise first; then we who are alive, who are left, shall be caught up together with them in the clouds to meet the Lord in the air; and so we shall always be with the Lord" (1 Thess. 4:16, 17, R.S.V.).

These texts, and many others like them, constitute the scriptural foundation for the blessed hope. Adventists believe Jesus is coming again because He said He would return. His second coming will be the consummation of the plan of salvation. It will be then that the millions who have been saved by grace will receive the eternal life promised in John 3:16. This will be one of the greatest events in the history of the universe.

These texts, and others like them, reveal the nature of the second coming of Jesus. It will not be a "secret rapture." It will not be the establishment of a kingdom in Palestine. It *will be* a great resurrection day. Those who have died in faith through the ages will be awakened to eternal life. Those who are living in Christ will be caught up "to meet the Lord in the air." Man is not naturally immortal. The idea that people continue to live after death was borrowed from Greek philosophy. Eternal life is a gift of God, and it will be bestowed when Jesus comes again. Paul tells the story with great clarity in the famous "resurrection chapter"—First Corinthians 15:

"But the truth is that Christ has been raised from death, as the guarantee that those who sleep in death will also be raised. For just as death came by means of a man, in the same way the rising from death comes by means of a man. For just as all people die because of their union with Adam, in the same way all will be raised to life because of their union with Christ. But each one will be raised in his proper order: Christ, first of all; then, *at the time of his coming,* those who belong to him. *Then the end will come"* (verses 20-24, T.E.V.).

At this point it would be well to raise the question: "Why are some people interested in the return of Jesus?" Could it be that when things are going well, people would rather not think about His second coming? But when they are sick, bankrupt, bereaved, harassed, or old, they turn to the blessed hope as a compensation for what they don't have in this life. One author writes as follows regarding those whose hopes are based on unworthy motives:

"Those who look to Christian hope as [being in itself] a compensation have a fragile hope because it depends on human circumstances. What we lack today we might receive tomorrow. Prosperity diminishes or makes unnecessary such hope. Hope then becomes only a wish projection of the deprived. We grow beyond such hope when we become better educated and better employed. Our earthly mansions can take the place of our heavenly, our Cadillacs for the heavenly chariots, our stylish wardrobes for the white robe of righteousness, our table delicacies for the tree of life. Because so many Christians view hope in such manner, their hope diminishes as their bank account increases."—Sakae Kubo, *God Meets Man,* p. 93.

Would it not be much more satisfying if Christians could look forward to the coming of Jesus *because they love Him* and want to be in His kingdom forever?

When will this great event take place? Jesus said He didn't know, nor did the angels in heaven know. Only His Father knew (Matt. 24:36). In the Bible, however, God has released information to help His followers know when Jesus' return is "near." Certain lines of prophecy reach their fulfillment. Certain "signs" point forward to the end of the age. Certain political and social conditions threaten the survival of the human race unless God intervenes.

It is not profitable to speculate on how near is "near" and how soon is "soon." Sometimes Christians forget that God loves the "world" as well as the "church." He is holding open the door of mercy until He sees that it would not serve the interests of His kingdom to hold it open any longer. Then the end will come. While He yearns to save every person, He will not allow this world to destroy itself with its bombs, smother in its smog, starve because of its overpopulation, or drown in its wastes. The day will come when He will have done all that is appropriate to be done for and through His church, and He will have done all that is appropriate to be done for His world.

The "blessed hope" is based on the great truth that God has the whole world in His hands.

Some complain that the doctrine of the second coming of Jesus makes believers insensitive to the needs and problems of people in this world. One of the best answers to this complaint was made by C. S. Lewis:

"Hope is one of the theological virtues. This means that a continual looking forward to the eternal world is not (as some modern people think) a form of escapism or wishful thinking, but one of the things a Christian was meant to do. It does not mean that we are to leave the present world as it is. If you read history you will find that the Christians who did most for the present world were just those who thought most of the next. . . . It is since Christians have largely ceased to think of the other world that they have become so ineffective in this. Aim at heaven and you will get earth 'thrown in': aim at earth and you will get neither."—*Mere Christianity,* p. 104.

"Are you determined to be personally ready to meet the Lord?" This is the second part of the vow. How do people become "ready to meet the Lord"? Articles two, three, and four of this baptismal vow have revealed the

answer. The believer accepts Jesus as his personal Saviour. He responds in faith to His amazing grace. He is adopted into His family. He accepts His forgiveness and responds to the transforming power of His Spirit. All this can happen in a moment of time, and at that moment he becomes "ready." If he should die, he would await the resurrection when he will see Jesus in His glory. If he should live until He returns, he will welcome Him as a long-expected friend.

Jesus said, "Be ye also ready" (Matt. 24:44). Note that He said, *"Be* ready," not *"Get* ready." Some seem to think they can wait until some unmistakable sign reveals that the return of Jesus is just around the corner—then they can make a feverish, last-minute preparation. That is not the message of the gospel.

There are those who are stimulated to action only by crisis. They hear a stirring sermon or read about some world crisis, and, moved by fear, they step up their religious activity. This is not "being ready." Jesus is coming for those who became "ready" when they accepted Him as their Saviour, and remained "ready" by never renouncing Him as their Lord. It is God who makes us "ready"; man cannot achieve readiness through his own efforts.

The baptismal vow speaks of being "determined" to be ready. This must be interpreted as a continuing and growing faith in the One who saved those who believe and who is returning to take them home. "Determination" is full commitment to the Lord. It is more than gritting one's teeth, giving up a few more of life's pleasures, attending a few more meetings, giving a few more dollars. Those who meet Him in peace will have found peace through faith, acceptance, surrender, commitment—and *love.*

Jesus reveals the secret of readiness. Matthew 24 and

GOOD NEWS ABOUT THE RETURN OF JESUS / 71

25 constitute a discourse by the Master Himself on His second coming. In Matthew 24 he establishes the fact that He *is* coming again, and in Matthew 25 He explains how to be ready. As was His custom, He made His points by telling stories—parables. In this case He told not one story, but three: the story of the girls who were unprepared, the story of the servant who was unprepared, and the story of the people in the last judgment who will be unprepared.

In the first story, Jesus told about ten girls who went to a wedding. As was the custom of the time, they took "lamps" so they could join in the celebration. But five of the girls took no oil for their lamps. The party began at midnight. Those who brought oil were ready—those who didn't plan ahead had to go in search of oil, and by the time they found some, it was too late.

What is the moral of the story? Don't wait until the final crisis to prepare to meet the Lord. *Be* ready—don't count on *getting* ready when the trumpet sounds! Maintain a close relationship with Jesus as Saviour and Lord *every day*. Trust Him, communicate with Him, serve Him, and you will be ready when He returns.

The second story was that of a man who went on a long trip. He called his three servants. To one he gave five thousand silver coins (T.E.V.), to another two thousand, to another one thousand. While he was gone, the first two servants worked hard and doubled their money. The third servant dug a hole in the ground and buried his. When the Master returned, he complimented and promoted the first two servants. Servant number three explained his failure by saying, " ' "I knew you were a hard man, and I was afraid you would rob me of what I earned, so I hid your money in the earth and here it is!" ' " (chap. 25:25, T.L.B.).

What is the moral of this story? This man had neither

love for, nor confidence in, his Master. With no motivation but fear, he was not ready for his Master's return. So if Christians are to be ready when their Master comes back, they must serve Him because they love and trust Him.

The third story is different. It is a dramatic picture of the final judgment, which will take place " 'when the Son of man comes in his glory.' " " 'Before him will be gathered all the nations, and he will separate them one from another as a shepherd separates the sheep from the goats' " (verses 31, 32, R.S.V.).

To the "sheep" on His "right" He will say: " ' "Come, O blessed of my Father, inherit the kingdom prepared for you from the foundation of the world; for I was hungry and you gave me food, I was thirsty and you gave me drink, I was a stranger and you welcomed me, I was naked and you clothed me, I was sick and you visited me, I was in prison and you came to me" ' " (verses 34-36, R.S.V.). The glorified Christ will explain His statement to the assembled nations: " ' "Truly, I say to you, as you did it to one of the least of these my brethren, you did it to me" ' " (verse 40, R.S.V.). The scenario goes on to describe the fate of those on the left, the "goats." They are consigned to destruction because they failed to respond to human need.

What is the moral of this story? Those who are ready when Jesus comes will be people who have deep compassion for other people and who reveal their compassion by acts of love.

This amazing chapter with its three stories illustrates another well-known statement of Jesus. He said, " 'You shall love the Lord your God with all your heart, and with all your soul, and with all your strength, and with all your mind [like the two faithful servants]; and your neighbor as yourself [like those on the right hand in the judgment scene]" (Luke 10:27, R.S.V.). *The way to be ready is to love.* The gospel is built on love—God's love for man, man's love for God, and man's love for his fellow man. When Christians promise to prepare to meet Him in peace, they are pledging their love, not only for Him but for His other children.

Article seven of the baptismal vow urges believers to "help others to be ready for His glorious appearing." Jesus said, " 'This gospel of the kingdom will be preached throughout the whole world, as a testimony to all nations; and then the end will come' " (Matt. 24:14, R.S.V.). He also said, " 'Go therefore and make disciples of all nations, baptizing them in the name of the Father and of the Son and of the Holy Spirit, teaching them to observe all that I have commanded you; and lo, I am with you always, to the close of the age' " (chap. 28:19, 20, R.S.V.).

As new believers make the vow to "help others be ready," how do they anticipate that they will fulfill it? The answer is *"However love may lead."* Some will find their principal area of witness in their homes, some in their business or profession, some in the outreach of the church, some in the neighborhood, some in the classroom, some in the pulpit, some at the writing desk, some in overseas mission service. Wherever and however they witness, their witness must not be that of the slave, scourged to serve, or of the schoolboy, seeking points on examination day. Their witness must be that of the disciple, filled with gratitude to Jesus about whom they are witnessing and with compassion for the people to whom they are witnessing. If they are willing to witness "however love may lead," they will be ready to respond whenever He calls them home.

The Pre-Advent Judgment. While not specifically mentioned in the baptismal vow, Adventist literature and preaching make frequent reference to a divine judgment to take place before the second coming of Jesus. This event is variously described as the "pre-Advent judgment," the "investigative judgment" or the "cleansing of the sanctuary."

The terms "pre-Advent judgment" and "investigative judgment" are synonymous. The first expression emphasizes the *time* of judgment; the second, the *purpose* of judgment. The Adventist understanding of this judgment is summarized in the following quotation from *The Seventh-day Adventist Bible Commentary:*

"In the investigative judgment the records of all who have at one time or another professed allegiance to Christ will be examined. The investigation is not conducted for the information of God or of Christ, but for the information of the universe at large—that God may be vindicated in accepting some and rejecting others. Satan claims all men as his lawful subjects. Those for whom Jesus pleads in judgment, Satan accuses before God; but Jesus defends their penitence and faith. As a result of the judgment a register of those who will be citizens of the future kingdom of Christ will have been made up."—On Dan. 7:10, p. 828.

Some people object to the idea that God needs to examine the candidates for heaven before Jesus comes to take them home. They say, "Were not these people accepted into the family of God when they became Christians? Isn't their salvation assured when they are born again?" Paul answers this question in his letter to the Colossian church:

"And you, who once were estranged and hostile in mind, doing evil deeds, he has now reconciled in his body of flesh by his death, in order to present you holy and blameless and irreproachable before him, *provided that you continue in the faith,* stable and steadfast, not shifting from the hope of the gospel which you heard" (Col. 1:21-23, R.S.V.).

The purpose of the *pre-Advent,* or *investigative,* judgment is to certify before the universe that those who are about to be saved are "safe to save." The saved will be those who have been redeemed because they responded in faith to God's amazing grace, and have "continued in the faith."

And now we must look at the phrase "the cleansing of the sanctuary." This phrase has been used by Adventists throughout their history to describe the pre-Advent investigative judgment. What does it mean?

The origin of the concept is found in the ancient Hebrew system of worship. After delivering Israel from Egypt, God directed the construction of a portable sanctuary to be the center of their worship. Their sanctuary consisted of a court and a tent with two apartments. Worship rituals took place in the court and the outer apartment, called the "holy place," every day of the year. The second apartment, or "Most Holy Place," was entered by the high priest only once a year for a special atonement service. Present-day Jews celebrate this ancient Day of Atonement as Yom Kippur.

The themes of Israel's worship were reverence for God and removal of sin. Day by day the sins of the people were figuratively transferred to the Most Holy Place. On the yearly Day of Atonement, the sins were figuratively removed from the sanctuary. This ritual was continued, with modifications, in the Temple built by King Solomon, and a later Temple built by Herod.

The New Testament book of Hebrews sees in these ancient rituals a symbol of the gospel of Jesus Christ. They are described as being "only a copy and shadow of the heavenly" (Heb. 8:5, N.E.B.).

"Fundamentally the lesson in the sacrifices is the same for Christians today as for those long-ago Israelites. As they needed a constant atonement for their sins and sinfulness, so do we. We are unceasingly in need of the blood of Christ to make us acceptable to God and for power to grow in the Christian life."—Thomas A. Davis, "Christ in the Old Testament Sanctuary," *These Times,* November, 1981, p. 4.

We have noted that the Old Testament ritual had its annual Day of Atonement. This was the time when the Israelites were cleansed from their sins. It was a bit like New Year's Day, when everyone started over with a "clean sheet"—everyone, that is, who believed in that which was taking place and who entered into the spirit of the service. For the cynics in Israel, it was a time of judgment and separation.

From their beginnings Adventists have seen the fulfillment of the Old Testament "cleansing of the sanctuary" in a prophecy found in Daniel 8:14—"Unto two thousand and three hundred days; then shall the sanctuary be cleansed." Without going into detail regarding the interpretation of this text, we can state that Adventists believe that the "sanctuary" is the dwelling place of God, of which Israel's sanctuary was a symbol, and that the "cleansing" of this "heavenly sanctuary" is the pre-Advent investigative judgment that will climax in the ultimate solution of the sin problem, the second coming of Jesus. An examination of the details of Daniel's prophecy has persuaded Adventist expositors that this "cleansing" began in 1844. In addition to His work as intercessor, Jesus, the heavenly high priest, assumed His function as judge in preparation for His second coming.

This interpretation of Daniel 8:14 has been coupled

with an emphasis by Adventists on Revelation 14:6, 7, which is a prophecy of the end-time: "Then I saw another angel flying high in the air, with an eternal message of Good News to announce to the peoples of the earth, to every race, tribe, language, and nation. He said in a loud voice, 'Honor God and praise his greatness! *For the time has come for him to judge mankind'* " (T.E.V.).

So the unique mission of the Seventh-day Adventist Church has been conceived from its beginning as the proclamation of the good news of salvation in the context of the pre-Advent judgment, and the imminent return of our Lord. This does not change the gospel, but it gives the message of salvation an urgency, a relevance comparable to that of John the Baptist when he proclaimed the message of the first coming of Christ. John's message was "Behold the Lamb of God" (John 1:36). The Adventist message is "Get ready to meet the Lamb of God." Both messages have been good news to those who accepted them, and have involved judgment upon those who rejected them.

This has been a very brief summary of an important and fascinating theme. For millions, this message has helped in the understanding of the meaning of the good news of salvation. Rightly understood, it brings new depth and meaning to the divine plan of redemption as it approaches its climax in the second coming of our Lord.

CHAPTER VIII

Good News About God's Gifts

"Do you accept the Biblical teaching of spiritual gifts, and do you believe that the gift of prophecy in the remnant church is one of the identifying marks of the church?"

THIS ARTICLE in the Seventh-day Adventist baptismal vow is often misunderstood. The idea of prophecy as a valid gift of the Spirit in the modern Christian church has not been generally accepted. One reason for the skepticism is that many individuals claiming the gift of prophecy have proved to be imposters or self-deluded enthusiasts. It is very important that persons anticipating membership in the Seventh-day Adventist Church have a clear understanding of what, in Adventist parlance, is called "the Spirit of Prophecy."

A search has been made throughout Adventist literature for an authority on this subject whose statements would accurately represent the theology of the church regarding spiritual gifts. From the several authors that might have been chosen, we have selected Francis M. Wilcox (1865-1951), for 33 years (1911-1944) editor in chief of the Adventist general church paper now known as the *Adventist Review*. Wilcox published a book in 1934 entitled *The Testimony of Jesus* in which he explains the Adventist viewpoint regarding this subject. We shall quote liberally from this book.

Wilcox explains the Biblical basis of the doctrine of spiritual gifts as follows:

"Since the close of the Sacred Canon, nearly two thousand years ago, there have been no additions to this compilation of sacred books. Very evidently, in the order of God, none will ever be made. The Holy Scriptures, as they have come down to us through the centuries, will constitute until the end of time the supreme standard of Christian doctrine and experience.

"But the closing of the Scripture canon did not mark the cessation of Heaven's communication with man. In His divine wisdom and foresight, Christ bestowed upon His church certain spiritual gifts for the edification and upbuilding of His followers. These gifts are enumerated by the apostle Paul as follows:

" 'Now there are diversities of gifts, but the same Spirit. And there are differences of administrations, but the same Lord. And these are diversities of operations, but it is the same God which worketh all in all. But the manifestation of the Spirit is given to every man to profit withal. For to one is given by the Spirit the word of wisdom; to another the word of knowledge by the same Spirit; to another faith by the same Spirit; to another the gifts of healing by the same Spirit; to another the working of miracles; to another prophecy; to another the discerning of spirits; to another divers kinds of tongues; to another the interpretation of tongues: but all these worketh that one and the selfsame Spirit, dividing to every man severally as he will.' 1 Cor. 12:4-11.

"The same Holy Spirit which inspired the Divine Word, known as the Bible, also reveals Himself to the

80 / THE GOOD NEWS

church through these spiritual gifts. There is, therefore, no discord or lack of harmony in these two methods of divine communication. The gifts do not take the place of the Word, nor does their acceptance make unnecessary the Scriptures of truth."—Pages 25, 26.

In further developing his thesis that "prophecy" is a valid and lasting gift of the Spirit, Wilcox quotes Ephesians 4:11-14, where Paul repeats, in effect, what he has said to the church at Corinth. These gifts, including prophecy, will continue to function in the church "till we all come in the unity of the faith, and of the knowledge of the Son of God, unto a perfect man, unto the measure of the stature of the fulness of Christ" (verse 13).

The next step in Wilcox' argument is as follows:

"This gift of prophecy, we affirm, has been manifested in the life and work of Mrs. Ellen G. White, connected with this movement from 1844 until the year 1915, when she was laid to rest."—Page 34. He lists seven "evidences" that Ellen White possessed the gift of prophecy promised to the church. These evidences, as Wilcox perceived them, may be summarized as follows:

1. Her writings are in harmony with Biblical teachings.

2. "Her writings are not set forth as an addition to the sacred canon."—Page 34.

3. Her leadership saved the church from mistakes, divisions, and doctrinal errors.

4. Her testimony was deeply Christian in its emphasis, and evangelistic in its outreach.

5. "Her messages make a direct appeal to the heart, and are proving in thousands of lives a transforming power, and an inspiration to Christian service."—Page 35.

6. Her personal life conformed to the standards of the gospel of Christ.

7. Her experience in receiving unique messages from God resembled those of the Biblical prophets.

Wilcox quotes Ellen White's own concept of her mission. She declared:

"I have had no claims to make, only that *I am instructed that I am the Lord's messenger;* that He called me in my youth to be His messenger, to receive His word, and to give a clear and decided message in the name of the Lord Jesus."—*Selected Messages,* book 1, p. 32. (Quoted on page 51.) Again Wilcox quotes from the same article: "I have written many books, and they have been given a wide circulation. Of myself I could not have brought out the truth in these books, but the Lord has given me the help of His Holy Spirit. These books, giving the instruction the Lord has given me during the past sixty years, contain light from heaven, and will bear the test of investigation."—*Ibid.*, p. 35. (Quoted on page 54.)

Many books? Yes! Nearly forty volumes came from her pen, plus thousands of articles and letters. This prolific literary output includes the well-known Conflict of the Ages Series—*Patriarchs and Prophets, Prophets and Kings, The Desire of Ages, The Acts of the Apostles,* and *The Great Controversy.* It includes such widely read books as *Steps to Christ, Thoughts From the Mount of Blessing, Christ's Object Lessons, The Ministry of Healing,* and *Education.* In addition there were many volumes of "Testimonies" dealing with specific personal and church problems.

Wilcox again denies that this library of books in any way supplants the Bible. He says:

"Not only should Mrs. White's writings be regarded as making no addition to the Bible, but only as they stand the test of the Sacred Canon can their claims be accepted. Indeed, it is by the Bible that the writings of Mrs. E. G.

White and of every other person claiming divine revelation are to be judged. The Bible is the great gauge, or rule, by which all other writings are tested and proved."—Pages 67, 68.

Wilcox' viewpoint on this issue carries special weight because he was a member of the original Board of Trustees of the Ellen G. White Estate. This board was the legal entity that held custody of her writings after her death. Wilcox was the last survivor of the original group of trustees.

Wilcox does not claim verbal inspiration for her writings. (By "verbal inspiration" we refer to the idea that the writings were dictated word for word by the Holy Spirit, much as a person would dictate to a secretary.) He quotes from a letter Ellen White wrote in 1906 to a church member who was concerned regarding the inspiration of her writings:

"In your letter you speak of your early training to have implicit faith in the testimonies and say, 'I was led to conclude and most firmly believe that *every* word that you ever spoke in public or private, that every letter you ever wrote under *any* and *all* circumstances, was as inspired as the Ten Commandments.'

"My brother, you have studied my writings diligently, and you have never found that I have made any such claims."—*Selected Messages;* book 1, p. 24. (Quoted on page 88.)

What, then, was Wilcox' conclusion regarding the place of Ellen White's writings in the lives of church members today? He wrote:

"On many occasions through the years she dealt with conditions in the church as they arose. Her instruction applied primarily to the day in which she lived and the conditions which were before her; but much of this instruction, the same as the instruction given to the prophets of old, had a more far-reaching application. To the extent that similar conditions might arise in the church in any future period, this instruction would apply with equal emphasis. Indeed, in much of the instruction that was given, the special application seemed to be to the closing days of the history of the church."—Page 132.

How about candidates for membership in the Seventh-day Adventist Church in the 1980s? Should they be expected to take a vow accepting Ellen White as a unique messenger of God to the Adventist Church? Few can base such an acceptance on personal acquaintance with her, because she died in 1915. Few can base such an acceptance on a *complete* knowledge of her writings, for the more than 100,000 pages of material are more than any average human being can read, let alone fully understand. Wilcox' counsel on this very pertinent question seems fair and reasonable:

"Inasmuch as the labors of Mrs. E. G. White have entered so largely into the development of the second advent movement, candidates for church membership should be made acquainted with the divine ministry to which she was called, and the influence of her labors and writings through the years. Opportunity should be afforded them to read her published books. When this instruction has been given candidates, but little question ever will be raised as to faith in the doctrine of spiritual gifts being made a test of church fellowship.

"If, as the result of this investigation, the one contemplating church membership arrives at settled convictions in opposition to this doctrine, he naturally will not wish to unite his interests with a church that holds it as a part of its religious faith. In any event he should be encouraged to wait until he has had time and opportunity

84 / THE GOOD NEWS

for more mature study of the question."—Page 137.

It is well to remember that Wilcox knew Ellen White during a great part of his adult life. He published *The Testimony of Jesus* nineteen years after her death. He had a remarkable privilege of observing her and her work both during her life and in retrospect. His carefully considered counsel is in harmony with Ellen White's own position. Her writings are intended as a source of spiritual enrichment and guidance. They can increase our understanding and appreciation of the Word of God and of Jesus, her Saviour and ours. But her writings are not a substitute for the Bible, and our loyalty to her is not intended to overshadow our loyalty to our Lord. She understood her mission to be that of "God's messenger." Her messages, rightly understood and applied, can enrich our lives, but they always take a secondary place to those of the Sacred Word. She describes the Bible as the "greater light" and her writings as a "lesser light" (*Colporteur Ministry,* p. 125).

The Bible mentions many people who possessed the gift of prophecy whose utterances were never part of the Scripture canon. There Nathan and Gad; Asaph and Shemaiah and Azariah; Eliezer, Ahijah, and Iddo. In the New Testament there were Simeon and Agabus and Silas. And there were women who had the gift of prophecy— Miriam, Deborah, Huldah, Anna, and the four daughters of Philip. We know little about most of these people, but God used them as His messengers to enrich the lives of His people at a specific time. It is not surprising that God has done it again! This is good news!

Any careful student of the writings of Ellen White will be impressed by her emphasis on Jesus and His saving gospel. In the *Comprehensive Index to the Writings of*

Ellen G. White there are eighty-seven pages of references under the heading of "Christ." Three of her books, totaling more than 1,500 pages, were devoted to the life and teachings of our Lord. The great truth of salvation through faith in Christ is the theme that recurs most often in her writings. She said, "We must present the law and the gospel together, for they go hand in hand. As a power from beneath is stirring up the children of disobedience to make void the law of God, and to trample upon the truth that Christ is our righteousness, a power from above is moving upon the hearts of those who are loyal, to exalt the law, and to lift up Jesus as a complete Saviour."—*Gospel Workers,* pp. 161, 162.

"A complete Saviour." He is the theme of Ellen White. He is the theme of Seventh-day Adventism. He is the hope of every Christian.

CHAPTER IX

Good News About the Church and Its Mission

"Do you believe in church organization, and is it your purpose to support the church by your tithes and offerings, your personal effort, and influence?"

"CHURCHLESS CHRISTIANITY" is a religious trend that has developed during recent years, particularly among young people. The advocates of this viewpoint want to be known as Christians, but they don't want to be identified with any organized church. They want to "do their own thing" without the constraints and responsibilities that go with corporate identity.

In article nine of the baptismal vow, the prospective Seventh-day Adventist is asked to "believe in" church organization and to support such an organization with money, effort, and influence. This is hardly a "churchless Christianity"!

Early Christianity was not "churchless." It had its roots in a group of twelve men, their divine Leader, and the people who accepted their teaching. Even the incomparable Christ did not carry on His mission alone.

After Jesus' ascension, 120 of His followers found a suitable headquarters in Jerusalem, spoken of as the "upper room." They prayed, they carried on some necessary business, such as filling the vacancy created by the death of Judas, and they waited for the promised Holy Spirit as directed by their Lord.

On the day of Pentecost about three thousand additions were made to the group of followers. These new believers "devoted themselves to the apostles' teaching and fellowship, to the breaking of bread and prayers" (Acts 2:42, R.S.V.). They were a learning, worshiping, and praying fellowship. The economic stress that overtook this group as a result of persecution was met by an organized welfare program. "And all who believed were together and had all things in common; and they sold their possessions and goods and distributed them to all, as any had need" (verses 44, 45, R.S.V.).

When the operation of the welfare program was threatened by a charge of racial prejudice in the care of Christian widows, the leaders of the church called a general meeting in which seven "deacons" were appointed and ordained to take care of the nonpreaching activities of the church.

It was not long until Christian churches began to be organized outside of Jerusalem. The most noteworthy of these was the one at Antioch in Syria. It was the first Gentile Christian church. The corporate identity of this church is revealed by the following comment: "For a whole year they [Barnabas and Paul] met with the church, and taught a large company of people; and in Antioch the disciples were for the first time called Christians" (chap. 11:26, R.S.V.).

Paul accepted God's call to be the messenger of Christ to the Gentile world. Among the churches he established were the congregations in Thessalonica, Philippi, Corinth,

Ephesus, and Galatia. Paul's letters to these and other churches are known as his "Epistles," which constitute a large portion of the New Testament. These churches had their leaders—elders and deacons—who led out locally in the work and worship.

However, Paul looked at Christianity not merely as "churches" scattered here and there throughout the world, but as "the church." He uses the analogy of the human body to explain his understanding of the church: "For just as the body is one and has many members, and all the members of the body, though many, are one body, so it is with Christ. For by one Spirit we were all baptized into one body—Jews or Greeks, slaves or free—and all were made to drink of one Spirit.

"For the body does not consist of one member but of many. If the foot should say, 'Because I am not a hand, I do not belong to the body,' that would not make it any less a part of the body. And if the ear should say, 'Because I am not an eye, I do not belong to the body,' that would not make it any less a part of the body. If the whole body were an eye, where would be the hearing? If the whole body were an ear, where would be the sense of smell? But as it is, God arranged the organs in the body, each one of them, as he chose. If all were a single organ, where would the body be? As it is, there are many parts, yet one body. The eye cannot say to the hand, 'I have no need of you,' nor again the head to the feet, 'I have no need of you.' On the contrary, the parts of the body which seem to be weaker are indispensable, and those parts of the body which we think less honorable we invest with the greater honor, and our unpresentable parts are treated with greater modesty, which our more presentable parts do not require. But God has so composed the body, giving the greater honor to the inferior part, that there may be no

GOOD NEWS ABOUT THE CHURCH'S MISSION / 89

discord in the body, but that the members may have the same care for one another. If one member suffers, all suffer together; if one member is honored, all rejoice together.

"Now you are the body of Christ and individually members of it. And God has appointed in the church first apostles, second prophets, third teachers, then workers of miracles, then healers, helpers, administrators, speakers in various kinds of tongues" (1 Cor. 12:14-28, R.S.V.).

This does not sound like "churchless Christianity." Paul's analogy of the human body was relevant to the church at Corinth, to any other church, or to all Christian churches, taken collectively.

The use of the term *church* to include all Christians is especially obvious in Paul's letter to the Ephesians. He says, "Christ is the head of the church" (chap. 5:23, R.S.V.); "Christ loved the church, . . . that he might present the church to himself in splendor, without spot or wrinkle or any such thing, that she might be holy and without blemish" (verses 25-27, R.S.V.).

One of the reasons why Christ founded a church was that the mission of the believers could be accomplished in no other way. It is the business of the church to tell the world about a loving, compassionate God, to remind the world that Jesus saves, and to proclaim to the world that Jesus is coming again. While each individual Christian can testify to these truths, it takes organization to herald this message to the world. The good news cannot be proclaimed effectively by churchless Christians.

This organizational pattern must include the local church, the regional church (in the Seventh-day Adventist organization, the local conference, the union conference, and the division), and the worldwide church (called the "General Conference" by Adventists).

Only an organized church can carry on a missionary program throughout the world. Such an undertaking requires the concentrated effort of the entire church body, expressed through appropriate organizational machinery. Only an organized church can carry on a widespread evangelistic program, including radio and television. Only an organized church can operate a publishing program for the producing and distributing of gospel literature. Only an organized church can operate an educational system including elementary and secondary schools, colleges, and universities. Only an organized church can build hospitals, operate medical schools, and carry on a program of health education. Only an organized church can meet human needs such as disaster and hunger.

Activities such as these are dependent upon the united efforts of millions of individual Christians, made effective by an efficient organizational structure. The success of the organization is dependent upon the existence of a sense of mission on the part of the believers. This sense of mission must be more than a vague desire to do something good—it must have a sound theological foundation. It must be a work of faith, not a commercial enterprise. One of Adventism's leading authorities on the mission of the church has expressed it as follows: "It was . . . [the] conviction that Christ had entered upon His last phase of mission, namely, to bring about the restoration of all things through His work of judgment, that brought into existence the Seventh-day Adventist Church, now the most widespread single Protestant missionary movement in the world. These people believe that God has called them to participate in Christ's own mission to prepare the world for His imminent return. Their mission is to present the gospel in such a way, through a comprehensive mission approach, that every person on earth will see Christ as their Saviour, their Lord, and their Judge, and prepare for His soon coming. This is not the teaching of a set of doctrines, but a mission of restoration: the restoration of God's image in man and the putting away of sin; the restoration of God's holy law and of every principle of God's kingdom; the vindication of God's sovereignty and the defeat of everything evil, rebellious, and unholy.

"There is no room for trivialties here. This mission requires the church to go into every part of the world and it impels believers to cross every boundary: sociogeographic, cultural, political, and religious. The Seventh-day Adventist Church does not insist that only through its own witness Christ can make Himself known, but it cannot leave to others the witness to which God has called it. Adventists 'recognize every agency that lifts up Christ before men as a part of the divine plan for the evangelization of the world,' but they wish at the same time to bear their witness freely and openly in all the world."—Gottfried Oosterwal, *Ministry,* July, 1972.

It is one thing to accept this understanding of the church as God's approved agency for carrying a message to the world; it is another thing to translate this belief into practice. The church may sing, "I love salvation because it's free," but its members must remember that it costs money to send missionaries, to broadcast the gospel, to train workers for the church, to operate publishing houses, to carry on a medical program, to support churches, and to help carry the burden of the world's pain and hunger.

How does God expect the church to carry this tremendous load? In the Old Testament, He directed His church members to give a tithe (one tenth of their income), and freewill offerings. The prophet Malachi, author of the last book of the Old Testament, relayed the following message from God to His people at that time:

" 'Will man rob God? Yet you are robbing me. But you say, "How are we robbing thee?" In your tithes and offerings. You are cursed with a curse, for you are robbing me; the whole nation of you. Bring the full tithes into the storehouse, that there may be food in my house; and thereby put me to the test, says the Lord of hosts, if I will not open the windows of heaven for you and pour down for you an overflowing blessing" (Mal. 3:8-10, R.S.V.).

The same God who guided Malachi in his warning to Israel inspired Paul to promote a fund-raising effort to help hungry Christians in Jerusalem. He said, "He who sows sparingly will also reap sparingly, and he who sows bountifully will also reap bountifully. Each one must do as he has made up his mind, not reluctantly or under compulsion, for God loves a cheerful giver. And God is able to provide you with every blessing in abundance, so that you may always have enough of everything and may provide in abundance for every good work" (2 Cor. 9:6-8, R.S.V.).

Do not these two passages sound remarkably alike? They are both based on the principle of stewardship. Church members are responsible to God for their use of the property He entrusts to them. In spending their resources, He asks them to give priority to the needs of His church, and He promises a blessing to those who comply.

In harmony with this Biblical teaching, Seventh-day Adventists have stressed the giving of tithes and offerings. The tithe is dedicated to the support of the gospel ministry. Offerings are given for church maintenance, foreign missions, Christian education, building of churches and institutions, welfare services, and may other projects.

Sacrificial giving is strongly advocated, but members are free to determine their own response. No one needs to

GOOD NEWS ABOUT THE CHURCH'S MISSION / 93

know the amount of any member's gifts except the church treasurer and possibly the pastor. Giving is promoted by persuasion, not coercion. A high regard is given to organizational financial responsibility. Local churches, conferences, and institutions are directed by responsible committees, not individuals, and their finances are carefully audited.

What are the facets of life that a Christian pledges to Christ when he becomes a member of His church? "Wealth, effort, influence." He does not enter the church as an onlooker, but as a participant. He may not possess much wealth, talent, or influence, but God accepts and uses that which he dedicates to Him.

The success of the church has not been based on a few people who have given great wealth, expended great effort, or wielded great influence. There are only a few such. The real strength of the church, however, is dependent on *every* member's being sensitive to God's call to him and to God's guidance in the use of his wealth, effort, and influence, however limited they may be. "Love so amazing, so divine, demands my life, my soul, my all."

David Livingstone is quoted as having said, "I will place no value upon anything I have or may possess, except in relation to the kingdom of Christ. If anything I have will advance the interests of that kingdom, it shall be given away or kept only as by giving or keeping it I may promote the glory of Him to whom I owe all my hopes in time and in eternity." This is stewardship at its best. This is in harmony with the teachings of Jesus. The success of the church in proclaiming the good news is proportional, to a large degree, to the loyalty of members and leaders to this ideal.

CHAPTER X

Good News About the Body God Gave You

"*Do you believe that your body is the temple of the Holy Spirit and that you are to honor God by caring for your body, avoiding the use of that which is harmful, abstaining from all unclean foods, from the use, manufacture, or sale of alcoholic beverages, the use, manufacture, or sale of tobacco in any of its forms for human consumption, and from the misuse of, or trafficking in, narcotics or other drugs?*"

"*YOUR BODY is the temple of the Holy Spirit.*" This is a reference to 1 Corinthians 6:19. The wording in the baptismal vow happens to be identical to that of *Today's English Version* of the Scriptures. Several reliable versions translate the text "Your body is *a* temple of the Holy Spirit." (See R.S.V., N.I.V.) This statement reflects one of the most important theological insights of the New Testament.

The Greeks thought the body was evil. This idea was borrowed by many early converts to Christianity. In some cases the result was asceticism, in which the desires and instincts of the body were sternly suppressed. In other cases this same Greek notion was interpreted to mean that the body was of no importance and that the Christian therefore was free to do whatever he pleased with it. Some Christians confused this interpretation with "Christian liberty."

Theologian Oscar Cullmann sensed this problem, and in a book first published in 1958 said, "God is the maker of the body. The body is not the soul's prison, but rather a temple, as Paul says (1 Corinthians 6:19): the temple of the Holy Spirit!"—*Immortality of the Soul or Resurrection of the Dead?* p. 30. Cullmann was making this point in connection with his belief that the resurrection of the body is the gateway to immortality. The idea of the body as a temple not only relates to the resurrection but also involves the question of how we treat the body during this life.

Seventh-day Adventists would subscribe wholeheartedly to the principle of the sanctity of the human body as stated by evangelical expositor Charles Erdman: "Christians are not their own. They have been purchased by the precious blood of Christ. Believers, therefore, by the purity and holiness of their lives, should honor him to whom they belong. The whole passage [1 Cor. 6:12-20] indicates the unique teaching of Christianity in reference to the dignity and sanctity of the human body. Christian liberty is not to be interpreted as license to indulge in fleshly sins, nor yet is the highest spiritual attainment to be regarded as an excuse for the neglect or abuse of the body, which is to be regarded as a holy instrument of Christ, as a sacred temple for the indwelling of the Spirit of God."—*First Epistle to the Corinthians,* p. 64.

When Paul insisted that the body is a temple of the Holy Spirit, he was directing his remarks specifically at sexual sins. There were new converts from paganism in the church at Corinth who felt that such sins were not serious. Paul is meeting the problem by stating that fornication is a sin against the body that is unacceptable conduct for a Christian because the body of a Christian is intended to be a "temple" of the Spirit of God. This is part of the New Testament theology of man.

The late William Barclay, famous New Testament scholar, insists that sexual sin—"fornication"—is not the only sin that insults the body. Barclay declares, "Drunkenness might do the same."—*The Letters to the Corinthians*, p. 63. Seventh-day Adventists would agree. That is why they specifically mention "alcoholic beverages" in the baptismal vow. *The Adventist theology of man convinces them that a Christian has no right to abuse his liver and his brain with alcohol.* Adventists see such practices as out of harmony with the concept that the body is a temple of the Holy Spirit. Some would argue that drinking "in moderation" is acceptable. Alcohol is too dangerous a drug to be used as a beverage, even "in moderation." Its effects are too subtle, too unpredictable, too destructive, to justify the risk. True, many people drink without *obvious* harm. But millions impair their health, their homes, and their careers by ingesting a drug that can do no one any good and carries the potential of great harm.

Just as a Christian has no right to abuse his liver and his brain with alcohol, he also has no right to damage his lungs, his nerves, and his heart with tobacco. Research during recent years has proved beyond a reasonable doubt that tobacco affects health. Tobacco has shortened the lives of millions and has impaired the quality of life of more millions. This is sufficient reason for it to be "off limits" for the Christian who believes that his body is a temple of the Holy Spirit.

The baptismal vow also speaks of "unclean foods."

GOOD NEWS ABOUT YOUR BODY / 97

This raises questions that deserve careful and honest scrutiny. The reference is to the eleventh chapter of Leviticus, which lists certain meats that the Israelites were to consider "unclean," and therefore not to be eaten. This list includes animals that neither chew the cud nor are cloven-hoofed, water creatures not having fins and scales, and certain specifically designated birds and insects. This law regarding "unclean" foods was part of a larger code of laws defining various forms of "uncleanness." The term *unclean* seemed to be a label characterizing certain foods, certain things, and people under certain circumstances as *impure*. The impurity might by physical, moral, or ceremonial.

In later Judaism, the idea of uncleanness developed into a set of taboos, elaborated by endless legislation and tradition. The ideal of purity gave way to the notion of satisfying the demands of law. This was, no doubt, the reason why the New Testament changed the emphasis from "unclean" to "inappropriate for a Christian." In place of citing a ceremonial and legal code, the New Testament declares the sanctity of the body by calling it "a temple of the Holy Spirit" and by saying "whether therefore ye eat, or drink, or whatsoever ye do, do all to the glory of God" (1 Cor. 10:31).

Why, then, should Christians be concerned with the distinctions made in the Old Testament between "unclean" and "clean" meats? Adventist literature on this subject contains the following quotations: "Many articles of food eaten freely by the heathen about them were forbidden to the Israelites. It was no arbitrary distinction that was made. The things prohibited were *unwholesome*. And the fact that they were pronounced unclean taught the lesson that the use of injurious food is defiling. That which corrupts the body tends to corrupt the soul."—*The*

Ministry of Healing, p. 280. (Italics supplied.)

In other words, the distinction between clean and unclean meats was not originally intended as a ceremonial taboo. The foods were forbidden because they were "unwholesome." It was later that this common-sense approach was supplanted by a system of taboos.

God was protecting His ancient people when He told them not to use certain commonly available members of the animal kindgom for food. He understood the possible results to the health of His people if they were to eat these things.

The issue boils down to this: If certain meats were considered unwholesome fifteen centuries, and even earlier, before Christ, is it not a fair assumption that they are still unwholesome today? Perhaps Moses, under God's guidance, was centuries ahead of his time when he issued the dietary regulations of Leviticus 11. Perhaps the Adventist baptismal certificate would be better understood if article ten were to read "unwholesome foods" rather than "unclean foods." Such terminology would cover the items proscribed in Leviticus 11, plus many other foods that characterize the diet of modern society.

The Old Testament laws indicate that God is concerned that people refrain from eating things that are not best for them. Is not God still interested that His creatures should not impair the length and quality of their lives by wrong dietary practices? Seventh-day Adventists have traditionally maintained that God is concerned about our health and physical well-being. Abstinence from tobacco and alcoholic beverages is part of that program. Abstinence from the drugs characteristic of the contemporary drug culture is also very important. Many Adventists are vegetarians. Most Adventists do not drink tea or coffee. Much emphasis is given to physical exercise. A chain of health-care institutions and a health-education program is part of church life.

The following statements from *The Seventh-day Adventist Bible Commentary's* additional note on Leviticus 11 give a comprehensive picture of the Adventist interpretations of the Old Testament food regulations and of the general principles involved in religion and health: "God's dietary laws are not, as some suppose, merely negative and prohibitory. God intends that man shall have the best of everything. . . . He who created all things knows what is best for the creatures He has made, and according to His knowledge He gives counsel and recommendations. . . . What God forbids is not withheld in arbitrariness, but for the good of man. . . .

"Some insist that God is more interested in the soul of man than in his body, that spiritual values are superior to the physical. That is true, but it should be remembered that body and soul are closely interrelated, that the one powerfully affects the other, and that it is not always easy to tell where one begins and the other ends. Though we agree that the spiritual man is of supreme importance, we do not think that therefore the body is to be neglected. Such, indeed, was the philosophy of certain medieval 'saints' who mortified the body for the benefit of the soul; but that was not God's plan. He put body and soul together for the mutal benefit of each. . . .

"God's dietary laws are not arbitrary enactments that deprive man of the joy of eating. Rather, they are sound, sensible laws that man will do well to heed if he wishes to retain health, or perhaps regain it. On the whole it will be found that the food God approves is the same food men have found best, and that disagreement does not come in the things approved, but in the things forbidden. . . .

"The dietary principles of Leviticus 11, together with other sanitary and health regulations, were intended by a wise Creator to promote health and longevity. . . . Based as they are upon the nature and requirements of the human body, these principles could in no way be affected either by the cross or by the disappearance of Israel as a nation. Principles that contributed to health 3,500 years ago will produce the same results today.

"The sincere Christian considers his body to be the temple of the Holy Spirit. . . . Appreciation of this fact will lead him, among other things, to eat and drink to the glory of God, that is, to regulate his diet according to God's revealed will. . . . Thus he must, to be consistent, accept and obey the principles set forth in Leviticus 11."—Pages 756, 757.

So when one pledges himself to eliminate alcoholic beverages, tobacco, and unclean [unwholesome] foods from his life style, he is doing himself a favor. He is making himself free to be his best. He is not slavishly and blindly observing religious taboos; he is adopting a life style that will help protect him from diseases that bring pain and sorrow and death. This is good news.

Avoiding liquor, tobacco, and unwholesome foods is by no means the only rule of good health. Any practice that weakens the body or mind, that tends to produce disease and death, that reduces effectiveness and alertness, is out of harmony with the Christian ideal of the sanctity of the body. Worry, overwork, excessive stress, overeating of good food, unnecessary deprivation, lack of exercise—all of these things and many more are important in considering the well-balanced life. There is no set of rules that governs everybody's practices. Common sense is a particularly important virtue.

One final suggestion: A person can follow meticulously

article ten of the baptismal vow; he can abstain from alcoholic beverages and tobacco and unclean foods, he can be a complete vegetarian, he can eliminate fat and sugar from his diet, he can walk (or even jog) many miles each day, he can be up on everything written about health—and he may be nothing but a healthy sinner! "The kingdom of God is not meat and drink; but righteousness, and peace, and joy in the Holy Ghost. For he that in these things serveth Christ is acceptable to God, and approved of men" (Rom. 14:17, 18).

There is a gospel of health, but *health is not the gospel.* "*By grace* are ye saved through *faith.*" This is *the* good news. A healthy body may be a byproduct of a new life in Christ. This also is good news. John said to one his friends, "I wish above all things that thou mayest prosper and be in health, even as thy soul prospereth" (3 John 2).

A healthy faith, a healthy mind, a healthy body—these are all great blessings. When a person's body is "a temple of the Holy Spirit," he will respect the divine Tenant enough to avoid the sins of the flesh and practices that shorten and impair life. And this should not be an intolerable burden, because the indwelling Holy Spirit is our "Helper," committed to the enrichment of every facet of our lives.

CHAPTER XI

Good News About Christian Life Style

"Knowing and understanding the fundamental Bible principles as taught by the Seventh-day Adventist Church, is it your purpose, by the grace of God, to order your life in harmony with these principles?"

ARTICLES ONE through ten of the baptismal vow deal with "fundamental Bible principles as taught by the Seventh-day Adventist Church." These principles include a doctrine of God, a doctrine of salvation, a doctrine of law, a doctrine of divine revelation, a doctrine of the nature of man, a doctrine of last things, and a doctrine of the church. In discussing these doctrines, we have tried to avoid a cold, theoretical approach. We have tried to show the relevance of these doctrines to personal experience.

Article eleven underscores the importance of internalizing religion. Knowledge must result in feeling and action if it is to be a dynamic force in the life. Every believer must face the question "What kind of a person should I be as a Seventh-day Adventist Christian?"

Behavior patterns must go beyond the mere observance of religious rituals. Going to church, reading the Bible, paying tithe, observing the Sabbath, saying prayers, having family worship—all of these things are excellent and essential. But there is another dimension to being a Christian. This "other dimension" might be called "life style." Christians must recognize that the term *life style* may include the religious observances we have just mentioned. The following paragraphs enlarge this concept to include the great moral values of life.

Paul had much to say on this issue. Most of his letters were divided into two parts. The first part dealt with theology, the second part with moral values. As an example, let us review what he had to say to the church at Ephesus, a congregation he had pastored for three years: "Get rid of your old self, which made you live as you used to—the old self that was being destroyed by its deceitful desires. Your hearts and minds must be made completely new, and you must put on the new self, which is created in God's likeness and reveals itself in the true life that is upright and holy" (Eph. 4:22-24, T.E.V.). Here we have a picture of God "creating" a new self in His likeness. This reminds us of God's transforming work in the Christian's behalf—a work that will advance as rapidly as the believer permits, and will continue as long as life shall last.

What will be the results of the creation of this "new self"?

"No more lying, then! Everyone must tell the truth to his fellow believer, because we are all members together in the body of Christ. If you become angry, do not let your anger lead you into sin, and do not stay angry all day. Don't give the Devil a chance. The man who used to rob must stop robbing and start working, in order to earn an honest living for himself and to be able to help the poor. Do not use harmful words, but only helpful words, the kind that build up and provide what is needed, so that what you say will do good to those who hear you. . . . Get rid of all bitterness, passion, and anger. No more shouting or insults, no more hateful feelings of any sort. Instead, be kind and tender-hearted to one another, and forgive one another, as God has forgiven you through Christ" (verses 25-32, T.E.V.).

Note how Paul builds a picture of Christian life style as it reflects moral values. He describes a group of people who are radically different from the world around them. They tell the truth. They control their anger. They do not steal. They earn their living. They help the poor. They are careful of what they say. They are not hostile, but kind, gentle, and forgiving. What a miracle the grace of God had wrought!

But this was not all: "Since you are God's people, it is not right that any matters of sexual immorality or indecency or greed should even be mentioned among you. Nor is it fitting for you to use language which is obscene, profane, or vulgar. [*The Living Bible* paraphrases this: "Dirty stories, foul talk and coarse jokes— these are not for you."] Rather you should give thanks to God. You may be sure that no one who is immoral, indecent, or greedy (for greed is a form of idolatry) will ever receive a share in the Kingdom of Christ and of God" (chap. 5:3-5, T.E.V.).

Two of the greatest obsessions of our world are sex and money. Both of these are good in their place, but both are capable of misuse. We don't have to search far today to sense the prevalence of sexual immorality and greed. These elements have no place in the Christian code of morals. It should be observed that people who are horrified by sexual promiscuity may be very greedy. Paul condemns both of these sins in the same sentence.

Paul summarizes his appeal as follows: "So be careful

GOOD NEWS ABOUT LIFE STYLE / 105

how you live. Don't live like ignorant people, but like wise people. Make good use of every opportunity you have, because these are evil days. Don't be fools, then, but try to find out what the Lord wants you to do" (verses 15-17, T.E.V.).

Then he adds what seems to be an afterthought: "Do not get drunk with wine, which will only ruin you; instead, be filled with the Spirit" (verse 18, T.E.V.).

These statements reveal to us Paul's concern that the Christian church be made up of intelligent, alert, thoughtful, temperate people, with impeccable moral standards. He advocates a life style that would distinguish Christians from the rest of the world.

He goes on to discuss human relationships. He urges that husbands love their wives, and wives respect their husbands. He admonishes children to obey their parents, and to parents he says, "Do not treat your children in such a way as to make them angry. Instead, raise them with Christian discipline and instruction" (chap. 6:4, T.E.V.). Paul, although not himself a family man, recognized that the church of Christ would be no stronger than the families that constituted its membership. In fact, Paul uses the relationship of love and respect between husband and wife as a symbol of the relationship that should exist between Christ and His church.

A highly moral life style is most important for the Christian. There are those who have succumbed to the notion that the phrase "only believe" means that the Christian can adopt almost any life style that appeals to him. The Christian must never forget the divine imperatives revealed in God's Word. Also, the Christian will be keenly conscious of his influence, and he must be willing to go the second mile rather than to be a "stumbling block" to one of his fellow Christians who is less well informed than he.

The Christian cannot choose his life style wholly on the basis of current cultural norms. For example, if a given culture does not frown on bribery, tax evasion, premarital sex, or homosexuality, this does not mean that these practices are a viable option for the Christian.

Leonard Griffith, in his book *What Is a Christian?* states this issue very clearly: "The editor of a great newspaper published this prayer for a newly inaugurated President of the United States, 'O Lord, give him the courage, not of his convictions, but of Your commandments.' No man will ever really stand firm in the presence of evil unless he sees himself as a servant of God, and therefore sees evil for what it really is—the disobedience of God's law and the betrayal of His love. Is that not, after all, the whole basis of morality in our Western world? Why do we object to the publication of obscene literature? Why do we revolt against sexual promiscuity, drunkenness, dope addiction, swindling, embezzlement, and murder? Because these things are not socially acceptable? On the contrary, they may be very acceptable in some anti-God political regime. ... Or is it that they do damage to our personalities? On the contrary, there is a school of thought which believes that the greatest damage lies in repression and self-discipline. No, our society revolts against the great moral and social evils because these things are wrong, everlastingly wrong, and because to do them is to violate the moral laws which from the beginning of time have been written into the constitution of the universe, laws which cannot be violated with impunity."—Pages 99, 100.

We should add to Dr. Griffith's excellent statement that if "our society" should repudiate all of these timeless moral principles, it would still be the obligation of the church to hold onto them and live in harmony with them, whatever the cost.

This article of the baptismal vow contains a phrase that must not be overlooked: "by the grace of God." The adoption of a Christian life style is not something that can be done successfully without help. The Christian must remember that when he is "born again" he is fully accepted by God, completely forgiven of his sins, and he stands before God as if he had never sinned. This all happens through the grace of God. But God is not pleased to have these forgiven sinners whom He has adopted into His family ignore the life style He wants them to live. He does not want them to disregard Him, to dishonor their parents, to violate the Sabbath, to steal, to commit adultery, to murder, to tell lies, and to covet. So the same gracious God who saved the person from his guilt when he *became* a Christian puts forces into operation to help him to *be* a Christian.

God gives this new Christian a pattern—His law as interpreted and lived by Jesus Christ. He also makes available to him a power—the presence of Jesus Christ in his life. God delegates His Holy Spirit to be a Helper in meeting temptations and problems. He also provides forgiveness in case of failure. "My little children," John said, "I am writing this to you so that you may not sin; but if any one does sin, we have an advocate with the Father, Jesus Christ the righteous" (1 John 2:1, R.S.V.).

This process whereby the grace of God transforms a sinner's life style is an ongoing experience. God continues to work in the Christian's behalf as long as life lasts. The purpose is to make the Christian *more* honest, *more* loving, *more* pure, *more* responsible, *more* understanding. The Christian never reaches a point that new heights do not beckon him. He is always aware of his imperfections, but he is also aware of God's guidance, and he knows that God hasn't given up on him.

What are Christians like who have been "born again" and who through the grace of God are growing in the Christian life style?

They are not smug or self-righteous. They realize their weaknesses and their needs. They are aware of their dependence on Christ. And they welcome the confidence and support of their fellow-Christians.

They are easy to live with. They are continually learning the meaning of the text that says, "Love is patient and kind; it is not jealous or conceited or proud; love is not ill-mannered or selfish or irritable; love does not keep a record of wrongs; love is not happy with evil, but is happy with the truth. Love never gives up; and its faith, hope, and patience never fail" (1 Cor. 13:4-7 T.E.V.).

They are different from the unconverted. "Though homes break asunder every day through impatience and infidelity, yet a Christian home will be a center of forbearance and sacrificial love. Though he lives in a day of relaxed moral standards when voices from every direction shout in his ear urging him to live like an animal, yet the follower of Christ, because he is a follower of Christ, will accept voluntarily the discipline of Christian manhood. Though society abounds in frivolous, luxury-loving people, who care for no one but themselves, yet the Christian will have about him a serious and unselfish concern."—Griffith, *op. cit.,* p. 20.

Being a Christian makes a difference. Being a Seventh-day Adventist Christian makes a great difference. The people in the community where an Adventist lives may not know who are the Methodists, Baptists, or

Presbyterians, but they are quite likely to know who are the Seventh-day Adventists. The Adventist should be distinguished, not for his dietary habits, not even because of the day on which he worships, but for his humility, his compassion, his honesty, his Christlikeness, his generosity, his fairness, his decency. This kind of life style can be good news in a troubled world.

CHAPTER XII

Good News About Baptism

"Do you accept the New Testament teaching of baptism by immersion, and do you desire to be so baptized as a public expression of your faith in Christ and in the forgiveness of your sins?"

THERE ARE two vows that many people take at some time during their lives. One is the marriage vow. The couple stands before a minister or a justice of the peace, and each party promises to love and honor the other so long as they both shall live. After the vows have been taken, the official declares them husband and wife. This new relationship, attested by witnesses, is recognized by the state and blessed by the church, if the participants choose a religious service.

The other is the baptismal vow. The minister asks questions such as those we have been examining in this book. If the candidate responds affirmatively, the minister baptizes the candidate "in the name of the Father, the Son, and the Holy Spirit," and the church has a new member. The candidate has entered into a new relationship with God and with the church.

Both of these relationships were ordained by God.

Both were designed by Him to bring lasting happiness. Neither relationship can be broken without damage to the parties concerned. And both of the relationships are suffering from the secularization of our culture. Let us take a new look at the meaning and importance of baptism.

The Scriptures are so clear about the form of baptism that little needs to be said. The *Seventh-day Adventist Bible Dictionary* summarizes it well: "That immersion was the mode employed in New Testament times is clear from the meaning of the Greek term, from Bible descriptions of the performance of the ceremony, and from the spiritual applications made in the Bible respecting the rite. The term *baptizo* was used anciently to describe the immersing of cloth in dye, and of the submerging of a vessel in order to fill it with water. Its most obvious meaning when applied to Christian baptism is 'to immerse.' "—Page 113.

Merrill C. Tenney, an evangelical theologian, agrees: "The Greek verb *baptizo,* which has been transliterated rather than translated, means fundamentally to *dip, plunge, immerse."*—Carl F. H. Henry, ed., *Basic Christian Doctrines,* p. 257.

While it is important to understand the correct form of baptism, it is much more important to grasp its spiritual meaning. The most important statement we can make about baptism is that it is a *symbol of salvation.*

"In discussing the significance of baptism Paul points out that (1) as Christ died for sin, the Christian must die to sins; (2) as Christ, having died, was buried, so the Christian is symbolically 'buried' with Him in the watery grave of baptism; and (3) as Christ was raised from the grave, so the Christian is raised to newness of spiritual life."—*SDA Bible Dictionary,* p. 113.

Was this *really* what Paul said? Listen: "Don't you know that all of us who were baptized into Christ Jesus were baptized into his death? We were therefore buried with him through baptism into death in order that, just as Christ was raised from the dead through the glory of the Father, we too may live a new life" (Rom. 6:3, 4, N.I.V.).

Death, burial, resurrection—that was the sequence of events by which our Lord made provision for our salvation, and that is the sequence of symbols by which baptism commemorates that provision. But baptism must be more than a celebration. It marks the beginning of a *new life.*

Seventh-day Adventists join with most other Protestants in insisting that baptism is not a sacrament—it does not, of itself, save. *Jesus* saves, and baptism is a way of affirming and accepting that salvation. H. M. S. Richards, pioneer Seventh-day Adventist radio preacher, says: "There is salvation in Christ only, not in an ordinance. Nevertheless, baptism is not to be omitted any more than a marriage ceremony is to be omitted by those who are to unite their lives in matrimony. Remember this, a young man may love his sweetheart just as much before the marriage vows are taken as he does later, but it is the ceremony that makes them married. So a person may love God just as much before he is baptized as he does later, but it is by the ceremony of baptism that he makes his public confession of Christ and enters the Christian church."—*30 Sermons,* p. 76.

There is a very important phase of the new birth experience that must not be overlooked. Jesus said to Nicodemus, " 'Unless one is born of water *and the Spirit,* he cannot enter the kingdom of God' " (John 3:5, R.S.V.). This is Jesus' way of emphasizing that water baptism *must* be accompanied by the coming of the Holy Spirit into the

GOOD NEWS ABOUT BAPTISM / 113

new believer's life.

Ideally, this "baptism of the Holy Spirit" should precede baptism by water. Then the experience in the baptistry becomes a witness of an experience that has already taken place. But in real life it is sometimes the case that the person who is baptized does not understand the place of the Spirit in his life. Such persons are like the twelve disciples of John the Baptist in Ephesus whom Paul informed about the Holy Spirit (Acts 19:1-7).

A contemporary Christian tells how a person may be "born of water" but not of the Spirit, and the sad consequences of such an experience: "I myself gave my life to God as a young man. But I received or accepted nothing. During part of that first year I passed through a doleful experience. The only thing I could think of was what I had given up or relinquished to become a child of God. I had nothing to live for. I wanted to die.

"Fortunately, I did not die. If I had died, I am sure I would have been eternally lost. After nearly a year in this dismal state, I woke up, as it were. In addition to giving up the world, I now accepted Jesus. Now the Spirit came into my life; I was baptized with the Spirit. Through this experience life became new to me. Now I had something to live for. Life beckoned me with limitless opportunities of service for Christ. . . .

"After we have been baptized with the Spirit, upon our acceptance of Jesus as our Saviour from sin, God hopes that we shall continue on to be filled with the Spirit and give Him full control in our lives."—A. V. Wallenkampf, *New by the Spirit,* pp. 51-53.

Happy is the person who is "baptized of the Spirit" before or at the same time he is "baptized of water." Paul wrote to the Corinthians, "By one Spirit we were all baptized into one body—Jews or Greeks, slaves or free—and all were made to drink of one Spirit" (1 Cor. 12:13, R.S.V.). The results of this "baptism of the Spirit" are enumerated in Paul's letter to the Galatians, "The Spirit produces love, joy, peace, patience, kindness, goodness, faithfulness, humility and self-control" (chap. 5:22, 23, T.E.V.).

"Love," "patience," and "kindness" have to do with the Christian's relations with his fellow men. The Spirit-controlled person is compassionate, and he is unfailingly kind.

"Joy" and "peace" reflect the security the Christian enjoys in Christ. The Spirit-filled Christian is not morose and fearful. He has every reason for happiness and confidence. His joy is more than emotional excitement.

"Goodness, faithfulness, humility, and self-control" describe the stability that comes into the life of the person who has been baptized of the Spirit. He is not weak, he is dependable, he is not arrogant, and his life is disciplined. He is not pushed about by cultural influences.

In article eight we discussed the "gifts" of the Spirit. These are given to different people as the Holy Spirit sees fit. One Christian has one "gift"; another Christian has a different "gift." But all Christians should possess all the "fruits" of the Spirit. These will not be fully mature overnight. But the newly baptized Christian, like a healthy, growing plant, will produce appropriate fruits. As sunlight, soil, and water cause plants to bear fruit, so the Holy Spirit makes the Christian's life productive.

The baptismal vow describes baptism as a "public expression of your faith in Christ and in the forgiveness of your sins." This is why baptisms are usually held at church services or other public meetings. The new convert is "telling the world" that he believes that Christ died for his sins and has forgiven them all. He is "telling the world" that he accepts Christ not only as his Saviour but as his Lord. He is "telling the world" that he believes the risen Christ imparts to him a new life. He is "telling the world" that now he is a Seventh-day Adventist Christian. He is committing himself in the presence of witnesses, just as do the bride and bridegroom at a wedding.

Baptism and church membership are not something a person tries just to see whether he likes it. To renounce these vows is a giant step backward. Whatever the reasons may be, renunciation of one's baptismal vow resembles a divorce. Unless there is an unreserved reconsecration to Christ, life can never be the same again.

We emphasize: *Baptism of water and of the Spirit do not result in instant spiritual maturity.* Peter told church members in his day:

"You have been born anew. . . .

"Like newborn babes, long for the pure spiritual milk, that by it you may grow up to salvation; for you have tasted the kindness of the Lord" (1 Peter 1:23-2:2, R.S.V.).

Most people discover that "growing up to salvation" does not usually denote uninterrupted progress. Christian living has its ups and downs. These have been well described in Dick Jewett's *Orientation for New Adventists:* "The future looks bright, and I wish for you a happy beginning. Jesus loves you. You love Jesus. In fact, you love everybody. So it's smooth sailing from here on, right?

"Wrong! The truth is, the battle has just begun, and anything that can go wrong in the next few weeks probably will go wrong. First thing you know, your halo of good intentions no longer seems to fit quite right. Some of the old ways keep coming back, and the halo keeps slipping off."—Page 7.

Jewett proceeds to recommend Bible study, prayer, meditation, and loving service for others as ways to solve these problems. He continues: "Of course you will suffer growing pains ahead. . . . Don't be surprised if the car breaks down, or you lose your job, or your doctor explains that you have an ulcer, or other big problems suddenly surface. Perhaps somebody in the church criticizes you for an innocent mistake. Or you try witnessing to your non-Adventist brother-in-law, and he asks you a stumping question that you have never thought of before. Furthermore, you have gained twenty pounds since you gave up cigarettes, and you're tempted to go back to coffee because of morning headaches."—Page 9.

The answer to these problems is not in oneself, but from God: "Don't you think God has ever seen a sinner before? He knows all about you and still loves you. In fact, He loved you way back when you didn't care if God existed. You have always been loved by God. You don't have to prove anything to Him. You don't have to be better so that He will love you more. He cannot possibly love you any more than He already does!"—Page 12.

It is in this relationship of love that a Christian finds the solutions to life's problems. God loves His children and He understands their weaknesses. Trust, born of this love, will enable believers to accept the forgiveness, the transformation, the hope that He is endeavoring to give them. Just as love is the solvent in the relationship of marriage, so love "bears all things, believes all things, hopes all things, endures all things" (1 Cor. 13:7, R.S.V.).

"Be watchful, stand firm in your faith, be courageous, be strong. Let all that you do be done in love" (chap. 16:13, 14, R.S.V.).

CHAPTER XIII

Good News About the Church as a Place of Worship and Fellowship

"Do you believe that the Seventh-day Adventist Church is the remnant church of Bible prophecy, and that people of every nation, race, and language are invited and accepted into its fellowship? Do you desire membership in this local congregation of the world church?"

WHAT DO Seventh-day Adventists mean when they speak of themselves as "the remnant church of Bible prophecy"? Isn't such a claim a bit arrogant? How about other sincere, born-again Christians of other persuasions?

First, we should note that the idea of a "remnant" is very prominent in the Old Testament, where the term is used more than eighty times. It generally means "what is left over," "the rest," "residue." The basic meaning in the Bible is similar to our use of the word to describe the last end of a bolt of cloth.

A study of the Bible texts containing this word reveals that it often describes a small group of people who remain faithful to God in a time when the majority are ignoring Him. They are often the "survivors" of moral and spiritual catastrophe. Listen to the prophet Isaiah:

> "Ah, sinful nation,
>   a people laden with iniquity,
> offspring of evil doers,
>   sons who deal corruptly!
> They have forsaken the Lord,
>   they have despised the Holy One of Israel,
>   they are utterly estranged. . . .
> If the Lord of hosts
>   had not left us a few survivors [a remnant],
> we should have been like Sodom,
>   and become like Gomorrah" (Isa. 1:4-9, R.S.V.).

"A remnant will return, the remnant of Jacob, to the mighty God. For though your people Israel be as the sand of the sea, only a remnant of them will return" (chap. 10:21, 22, R.S.V.).

Paul quotes these passages in Romans 9:27-29. He also refers to the Old Testament experience of Elijah when God told him that there were seven thousand faithful worshipers of God in Israel, and Paul makes an application to his own day "So too at the present time there is a remnant, chosen by grace" (chap. 11:5, R.S.V.).

The unique Seventh-day Adventist application of the "remnant" idea is based on a passage found in Revelation 12:13-17, which is part of a prophetic picture of the efforts of Satan to destroy the church.

In this passage, the church is symbolized as a woman who gave birth to a child, representing Jesus. Immediately Satan, symbolized by a "great red dragon," endeavored to devour the child, who was "caught up to God and his throne." This, of course, represents the ascension of Jesus. The woman (the church) fled into the wilderness, where God protected her through long centuries of conflict. Finally the record says, "The dragon [Satan] was furious with the woman [the church] and went off to fight against the rest [remnant] of her descendants, all those who obey God's commandments and are faithful to the truth revealed by Jesus" (Rev. 12:17, T.E.V.).

The remnant represents a surviving minority—people who are not controlled by contemporary culture. They decide to obey God and accept Jesus as their Saviour. And the context of this passage indicates that this particular remnant will live during the final years before Jesus returns the second time.

So when Seventh-day Adventists speak of themselves as the "remnant church of Bible prophecy," they are designating themselves as a minority whose beliefs and practices distinguish them from the rest of the world. In what respects is this true?

Adventists observe Saturday as the Sabbath because of their conviction that people who have been saved by grace should respond to that grace by observing the commandments of God. The Adventist concept of God causes them to reject the common idea of an ever-burning hell. The Adventist idea of the sacredness of the human body causes them to avoid those foods, drinks, and drugs that would weaken and destroy the body. The Adventist doctrine of spiritual gifts causes them to accept the messages of Ellen White as a source of guidance for the "remnant" church. The Adventist sense of mission inspires them to carry their message to all the world. In the words of Revelation 12:17, T.E.V., Adventists insist that the Christian message includes *both* the commandments of God and "the truth revealed by Jesus." The theology blends redemption and responsibility.

These and other doctrines and viewpoints make Adventists different. This minority status sometimes causes personal problems. Some Adventists have to change jobs because they will not work on Saturday.

Some lose friends and are disowned by family because they are "different." This is part of what it means to be a member of a minority religious group.

Joining a minority church does not mean that Adventists repudiate those who do not agree with them. They recognize that there are many sincere Christians in all communions who love God and whom God loves. But Adventists believe that God has a unique work that He wants done, a unique message He wants preached, and that He has asked Adventists to do this work and preach this message. It is not their business to judge others who do not share their beliefs; it is rather their business to witness for their faith.

It is possible for members of a minority faith to become paranoid—to develop a persecution complex, to live in a state of hostility and fear. Such is *not* God's plan for His remnant. A popular magazine was once advertised by this slogan: *"Vogue is read by the overwhelming minority."* The members of a minority church must neither be apologetic or arrogant.

Adventists are not a "cult." They accept Jesus as their Saviour in the most evangelical sense. They are Christians, but they are unique in that they emphasize certain beliefs and duties that they believe the Christian world is neglecting. They invite the whole world, regardless of nationality, race, class, and language, to join them in the fellowship of this "remnant" church.

It is particularly important for a minority religious group to enjoy a close fellowship among themselves. They especially need this fellowship because they don't always "fit" in the contemporary culture. This does not mean that they should withdraw themselves from the world. Their best witness is a warm, friendly relationship with their neighbors. But their fellowship with those who share their beliefs, their interests, their life style, and their hopes is one of the compensations of being a part of the "remnant."

This Christian fellowship must revolve around worship. Fellowship without worship may be secular; worship without fellowship may lack the human touch. It is true that a person can worship God by himself, or two or three people can worship in a home. But throughout the entire Bible, there is emphasis on group worship, the adoration of God by a congregation. Worship is the one unique and indispensable activity of the church.

> Beautiful is the large church,
> With stately arch and steeple;
> Neighborly is the small church,
> With groups of friendly people;
> Reverent is the old church,
> With centuries of grace;
> And a wooden church or stone church
> Can hold an altarpiece.
> And whether it be a rich church
> Or a poor church anywhere,
> Truly it is a great church
> If God is worshiped there.
> —Author Unknown

The effectiveness of worship is dependent upon the depth of the Christian experience of each worshiper. Only a redeemed person can really worship God, because worship is a redeemed person's response to his Redeemer. There is a certain behavior pattern that will characterize the true worshiper as he goes to the place of worship on the Sabbath day:

1. He will enter the sanctuary quietly and on time.

2. He will sit quietly and thoughtfully while waiting for the service to begin.

3. He will, to the best of his ability, participate in the hymns and the responsive Scripture lesson.

4. He will concentrate on the prayers.

5. He will contribute as he can to the offering as a part of worship.

6. He will listen to the anthems and the special musical numbers with an attempt to sense their message.

7. He will give undivided attention to the sermon.

8. He will make it his personal responsibility to avoid any distractions or disturbances that would break the reverent silence of the house of worship.

9. He will remember that God's presence is not only in the pulpit but in the heart of each worshiper.

10. He will leave the sanctuary quietly and reverently.

The fellowship of worship is enhanced by the joy of just being together. A Christian can feel quite alone as he fights to survive in a secular world, but the services of the Sabbath day can be like a strip of blue sky with the sun shining through. There is fellowship in the Sabbath School class, in the communion service, at the baptismal service, at the church potluck, or common meal. There is fellowship at the baby dedication, the wedding, the funeral. The most important happenings in life are celebrated by the church. No place stimulates memories like the church. Nothing can banish loneliness like the warm, understanding fellowship of the church.

Ideally, the church is a place where there are no barriers. "The ground is level at the foot of the cross." Color, education, occupation, wealth—all of these things are incidental when individuals kneel before God and extend the hand of fellowship to one another.

Every perceptive person recognizes that the church—yes, the Seventh-day Adventist Church—falls short of the ideals Jesus has for it. Some people allow the imperfections of the church to be a stumbling block. They forget that it is made up of *people* with all their weaknesses. Every person who enters the church should do so with a determination not just to *receive* fellowship, support, sympathy, and encouragement, but to *give* such blessings to his new brothers and sisters. The grace of understanding and forgiveness is essential to fellowship. Members need to help one another in the development of these virtues.

The four primary ingredients of life are worship, work, love, and play. Baptism into church membership can be the gateway to a full appreciation of the experience of worship; a new relationship to God may add a new dimension to work; the love that is the essence of the gospel may penetrate every relationship of life; even recreation may be repatterned so that it will re-create rather than destroy.

Dr. John R. W. Stott has written a book, based on Jesus' Sermon on the Mount, in which he describes Christianity as a "counterculture." This is a very apt description. Seventh-day Adventism is, in a sense, a subculture within a counterculture. While Adventism is basically in agreement with evangelical Christianity, it has certain beliefs and practices that are unique. And Adventists believe these points of difference to be very important. This makes the Biblical term *remnant* an appropriate term to describe the Adventist movement. Adventists are concerned that their message needs to be heard in a world moving toward the return of Jesus. And they invite people everywhere to join them in this mission.

Epilogue

WHEN A person becomes a naturalized citizen of a country, he must affirm his allegiance to his adopted homeland, and he should possess a basic understanding of the privileges and duties of citizenship. But this is only a beginning. Such a person could, if he wished, spend the rest of his life studying the history, geography, and institutions of his new homeland.

So with the newly baptized Seventh-day Adventist Christian. The vow he takes and his baptism have admitted him into the fellowship of the church. A lifetime of living and learning lie ahead.

First of all, being a Christian is a daily fellowship with God. New insights and achievements come as his understanding broadens and his commitment deepens.

Also, many new people will come into his life. These new friends, acquaintances, and associates can be a great blessing to him. But they aren't perfect.

His life will take on new patterns. He will doubtless be involved in some of the activities of his church—Sabbath school, youth, Community Services, leadership, witnessing. If he has children, he will face the realities of Christian education. He will develop new social and recreational patterns. Even his occupational patterns may change. He may recall the words of Paul: "All things are become new" (2 Cor. 5:17).

There is a vast area of Christian growth open to every member. In addition to Bible study, there are the many volumes written by Ellen White that will challenge his attention. There are the current church periodicals such as the *Adventist Review*. The Adventist Book Centers are filled with a wide variety of books from which he can select items of interest. All Adventists can profit by increasing their acquaintance with Adventist history, doctrine, and institutions.

His life will not be dull. In addition to family, community, and occupational interests, he now is a part of a dynamic church with a well-defined program. Sometimes he may feel driven. Here again, he will need to exercise common sense in balancing the various facets of his life.

The Seventh-day Adventist Christian should make no provision for spiritual failure. Acceptance of Jesus as Lord and Saviour should be a lifetime commitment. The baptismal vows should not be short-term, negotiable promises but, like the marriage vow, should endure as long as life shall last. The life style should be consistent, with flexibility in areas where no principle of right and wrong is involved. The weaknesses and mistakes of fellow church members should never be an excuse for breaking the ties of church fellowship. The once-for-all experience of the new birth should be followed by a once-for-all commitment to the new life.

The ultimate source of success and satisfaction in his new venture will be prayer. It has been said that "prayer is a fight for the power to see and the courage to do the will of God."—Harry Emerson Fosdick, *The Meaning of Prayer,*

p. 162. The lasting value of the vow he is taking will be proportional to the relationship that exists between him and God.